MINDFULNESS LIVING

Achieve Happiness With 100 Meditations For the Soul

MARINA MANNING

Copyright © 2020 Marina Manning

All Rights Reserved

Copyright 2020 By Marina Manning - All rights reserved.

The following book is produced below with the goal of providing information that is as accurate and reliable as possible. Regardless, purchasing this eBook can be seen as consent to the fact that both the publisher and the author of this book are in no way experts on the topics discussed within and that any recommendations or suggestions that are made herein are for entertainment purposes only. Professionals should be consulted as needed prior to undertaking any of the action endorsed herein.

This declaration is deemed fair and valid by both the American Bar Association and the Committee of Publishers Association and is legally binding throughout the United States.

Furthermore, the transmission, duplication or reproduction of any of the following work including specific information will be considered an illegal act irrespective of if it is done electronically or in print. This extends to creating a secondary or tertiary copy of the work or a recorded copy and is only allowed with express written consent from the Publisher. All additional right reserved.

The information in the following pages is broadly considered to be a truthful and accurate account of facts and as such any inattention, use or misuse of the information in question by the reader will render any resulting actions solely under their purview. There are no scenarios in which the publisher or the original author of this work can be in any fashion deemed liable for any hardship or damages that may befall them after undertaking information described herein.

Additionally, the information in the following pages is intended only for informational purposes and should thus be thought of as universal. As befitting its nature, it is presented without assurance regarding its prolonged validity or interim quality. Trademarks that are mentioned are done without written consent and can in no way be considered an endorsement from the trademark holder.

Table of Contents

Introduction 8

PART I 10

    Chapter 1: Back to the Basics 11

    Chapter 2: Unlocking Your True Purpose Through Mindfulness 15

        Re-centering Yourself 15

        Giving Your Emotions Space 17

        Making Clear Decisions 18

        Keeping Yourself Safe 18

        Improving Relationships 19

        Fostering True Joy 21

    Chapter 3: Moving Mindfully in Daily Life 23

        Coming to the Present Moment: Daily Guided Mindfulness Meditation With Journaling (Week 1) 23

        Coming to the Present Moment: Daily Guided Mindfulness Meditation With Journaling (Week 2) 27

        Coming to the Present Moment: Daily Guided Mindfulness Meditation With Journaling (Week 3) 29

        Mini Meditation Toolbox: 15 Quick and Easy Meditations to Integrate Mindfulness Into Your Daily Life 32

        Mini Meditation Toolbox: 10 Quick and Easy Meditations to Ease Stress, Depression, Addiction, Anxiety, Pain, Distraction, and Loss Using Mindfulness 41

PART II 48

    Chapter 1: Energy Healing- The Key to Holistic Health 49

    Chapter 2: Energy Healing and Overcoming Suffering 52

        Energy and Grief/Trauma 52

Energy and Mental Health 53

Daily Energy Regulation 54

Chapter 3: The Daily Energy Healing Journey 56

Understanding Your Energy Field: Daily Energy Healing Meditation with Journaling (Week 5) 56

Protecting Your Energy Field: Daily Energy Healing Meditation with Journaling (Week 6) 58

Healing Through Trapped Emotion Release: Daily Energy Healing Meditation with Journaling (Week 7) 59

Cultivating Self-Trust in your Healing Journey: Daily Energy Healing Meditation With Journaling (Week 8) 61

Mini Meditation Toolbox: 25 Quick and Easy Energy Restoration and Protection Meditations 63

Conclusion 80

Chapter 1: The Clutter in Your Life 124

Why You Have Clutter 125

You Don't Recognize What Clutter Is 125

You Don't Know How Long You Should Keep Something 126

You Don't Know How to Store Things 126

You Are Not Using Clutter Busters 127

Buying Too Many Things, You Don't Need 127

You Can't Let Things Go 128

Endowment Effect 128

The Consequences of Too Much Clutter 129

Your Stress Levels Increase 130

Your Diet Is Impacted in A Negative Way 130

You Can Develop More Respiratory Issues 130

Your Safety Is Threatened 131

Your Love Life Is Jeopardized 131

Your Kids Will Be Upset 132

  You Will Become Isolated 132

  You Will Miss Out On Getting Promoted 132

  You Are More Likely to Miss Work.. 133

  Your Productivity Decreases.. 133

  You Will Develop Poor Spending Habits.. 134

  You Can Go into Debt... 134

 Clutter is Not Just Physical.. 135

Chapter 2: Breaking Your Relationship With "Stuff" 137

 Getting Over the Endowment Effect.. 137

 More Decluttering Tips... 138

 Stop Buying Stuff You Don't Need 140

 The Benefits Of Decluttering 143

 Decluttering Equals Increased Focus and Productivity 144

 Decluttering and Improved Health 145

  Improved Healthy Habits 145

  Better Self-Care... 146

  Losing Weight... 146

  Easier to Relax 147

 Having More Space 147

 6-Week Decluttering Challenge 148

 ^ 150

 Chapter 4: The Many Types of Yoga 165

Introduction

Humans, at the core, are energetic beings. Throughout our lives, it is very easy for our energies to become out of balance due to traumatic events, grief and loss, and daily stressors, which are often a result of unhealthy societal and cultural expectations. If you look closely at yourself and other people and feel like something seems to be missing, the information in this book is for you.

This book will address three parts of the whole, which are crucial to healing the entire being on an energetic level: Mindfulness, Chakras, and Energy Healing. Each section will be followed by Guided Meditations and Journaling opportunities so you can adequately process what you are learning and keep track of how it impacts your experience. Additionally, the book contains a toolkit of 50 mini-meditations to give you a place to start and keep you on track in your journey. The information within these pages will demonstrate the flaws in the general population's approach to health; true healing is not possible without understanding all parts of the whole. This book will describe what healing looks like on a molecular level and revolutionize the way you consider health and healing. You will be given all the tools you need to check in with yourself, monitor and nourish your energies, return to the present moment, heal from the pains of your past, and ultimately, return to your highest self.

PART I

Finding Your Way Back to the Present Moment

Chapter 1: Back to the Basics

When most people think of mindfulness, they envision monks or yogis, sitting cross legged for hours with closed eyes and poised fingers overlooking the Himalayas. Although mindfulness is present in the lives of monks and yogis, what most people don't know is how easy it is to incorporate mindfulness into our everyday lives. As a matter of fact, a mindful state is the most natural and restful state for human beings—a state in which we were all living and moving in as children. If you think back to your childhood, you will likely remember that your concept of time and perception of reality was much different. Most children are very in touch with their emotions, letting them come and go naturally. If a child falls down in one moment and skins their knee, the child will likely begin to cry. However, if a few moments later they are being offered ice cream, their tears will dry, and they will continue on with their day. Mindfulness is the reason children are so in tune with the details of life that adults seem to miss. It is also the reason they are more likely to screech with joy, run around excitedly in enjoyable environments, wake up easily in the morning, and take the time they need to calm down from anger or sadness until the next happy moment arises. Children spend very little time thinking about things beyond the present moment. Even if they have something to look forward to, they are still likely to become invested in the moment at hand, whether that is playing, enjoying time with their parents, or eating a meal. So, what happens as people grow older that brings us away from this natural state of mindfulness?

There are a number of factors that pull people out of the present moment. From the time a child begins elementary school, they are presented with a schedule for the day, which remains relatively the same. Children are expected to remain within the structures presented to them, and the idea of forward-thinking and preparing for the next hour's activity becomes introduced. As they grow, children will likely have more expectations placed upon them, whether those expectations are academic, extracurricular, or within the home. Of course, it is necessary for children to learn how to be responsible and dedicate the time they need to the important things in life. However, as they become further exposed to the constant rush and future-oriented thinking of their parents and teachers, they come to see time as something that no longer belongs to them to fully inhabit.

Furthermore, as people approach teenage and young adulthood, they will begin to face challenges that most children are either shielded from or otherwise unaware of. People become flooded with the pressure to perform well and always be doing more today than yesterday. Although the expectations of cultures and societies vary, we can be sure that people are overwhelmed with the pressure to meet those expectations in order to be considered successful and valid. Once one bar is crossed, another one is waiting, and there is no time to slack. Additionally, the older people become, the more likely they are to be subject to long-lasting pain in their lives. This can come in the form of relationships ending, failing to accomplish something, being mistreated by other people, losing and grieving loved ones, or coming to terms with painful childhood events that did not make sense at the time. Teenagers become increasingly subject to mental health issues as they advance into adulthood, having to face all of the hard realities of the world and still come out on top. People may also be subject to trauma as a result of illness, accident, or abuse. All of these factors are enough to work against people and pull them out of the present moment, either because it is too painful to be there, or because they are simply too distracted.

Human beings experience over 60,000 thoughts per day, but the vast majority are dedicated either to planning for the future or worrying about the past. Becoming overly concerned about the future or steeping in the pains or regrets of the past can increase levels of stress in the body, which makes people more anxious and prone to physical health problems.

The mind naturally wanders, and it is impossible to keep thoughts from coming. Mindfulness is not a tool to eradicate such thoughts, as is the common misconception. Rather, it is a tool through which to acknowledge the thoughts the mind creates, bring attention to them, and allow them to move through. This ultimately brings people into what is happening here and now and gives them more control over their minds and how they orient themselves in their environments.

Because mindfulness is a skill that all human beings are equipped with at our core, it is something that can be re-learned. Just as we exercise our bodies to strengthen our muscles, so we must work to strengthen our brain through mindfulness. The way this strengthening happens is through being aware of thoughts as they arise, then breathing back into the present moment. The more practice is given to returning to the present moment, the stronger the mind will become in remaining in the present more often. Just as the body physically strengthens and becomes healthier over time with exercise, mindfulness exercises can physically change the structure of the brain to make it healthier. Mindfulness activates the positive components of the hippocampus, which is the part of the brain responsible for good things like creativity, joy, and the ability to process emotions. This, in turn, decreases stress levels, depressive tendencies, addictive behaviors, and the fight or flight instinct by shrinking the part of the brain responsible for negative things (the amygdala). Overall, increased mindfulness is the key to a longer, healthier, more creative, and more joyful life.

Chapter 2: Unlocking Your True Purpose Through Mindfulness

Re-centering Yourself

Everyone has days where everything seems to be spinning out of control, and there seems to be no way to manage the chaos. The days where you wake up late, run late to work, spill coffee on your shirt, get cut off on the road, get yelled at by your boss, spend the entire day at work in a confused frenzy, only to come home and bicker with your partner. Since the beginning of time, the human mind has been conditioned to release stress hormones and illicit the fight or flight instinct for the purpose of protection and survival. In the past, this primal instinct was very useful for escaping threats. As times have changed, the threats have become less severe, but the brain's response has remained largely the same. Now, these fight or flight reactions are likely to be triggered by everyday scenarios, such as those previously detailed. The hormone-induced responses that occur when we're stressed out are quick to send us spiraling into emotionally dramatic, and far less peaceful dimensions.

The good news is, mindfulness can be used as a tool for re-centering and gaining control over your anxiety and emotional reactions when you start to feel yourself spiral. Although there is no way to avoid stress and drama in daily life, mindfulness can serve as a shield of calm presence to protect your well-being. If you are preparing to enter a situation that you anticipate could be stressful, like a high-stakes day at work, a scary doctor's appointment, or a difficult conversation with a loved one, it can be incredibly helpful to bring yourself down to a more calm and balanced state in preparation for the stress you are about to deal with. You may find yourself with a racing heart, sweating palms, an unclear head, and the feeling of "butterflies in your stomach." Another area where it is common to feel these physical effects of anxiety is when encountering dramatic situations. Drama can arise tense moments with other people, as well as within the theoretical situations people create for themselves when worrying about what they cannot control (for example, the perception other people have of them, or events that may or may not occur in the future). Giving attention to what is happening in your mind and body and allowing yourself to breathe into the moment can be a total lifesaver in moments of drama or stress. Two to three minutes of deep breathing in your car before going to work, or taking a few deep breaths before reacting in a tense moment, can make a drastic difference in your sense of balance and your ability to deal with stress without launching into fight or flight.

Giving Your Emotions Space

The goal of mindfulness is not to eliminate emotions, but rather, to gain control over the impact they have on how we orient ourselves in the world. It is vital to honor our emotions and give them space to exist and teach us, without letting them seize control. Mindfulness is an excellent tool for giving our emotions space in this way. When an emotion arises, mindfulness gives us a chance to observe that emotion without judgment. In this calm space, we can ask our emotions, "What are you trying to teach me?" We can more clearly discern why we are experiencing a certain emotion, and become in touch with the deeper needs that may have caused that emotion to arise. Just as a child may cry when they need to be nourished our held, we may find ourselves growing angry or agitated when we need support, touch, or self-care. Similarly, we may find ourselves feeling stressed or anxious in scenarios that are subconsciously triggering moments from the past. In these cases, our stress and anxiety are begging us to become in touch with our past self, reminding ourselves that we are safe, and the traumatic moments from the past are over. Once our emotions have been given a non-judgmental space to exist, they can smoothly and peacefully move through the body and be released. This frees us to move from moment to moment like children do, without being constrained by unresolved emotions. Additionally, giving this space to our emotions in mindfulness helps to temper our reactions, which can prevent us from acting out in extreme ways and potentially doing or saying something we regret.

Making Clear Decisions

With the human mind constantly being muddled with thoughts, it can be hard to see things clearly. Sometimes our minds are cluttered by the expectations flying at us from every different direction, or perhaps by our fears of what will happen if things don't go to plan. When it comes to making decisions, we are often faced with numerous options, and it can be difficult to navigate through the chaos in our minds to come to a well thought out resolution. In a distracted, anxious, or removed state, our minds are like a pond on a rainy day—rippling to a point where there is no more clarity. Mindfulness is the calming of the waters, which brings us to a place where we can more clearly think of all possible outcomes of a decision and check in with what we truly need before moving into the next moment.

Keeping Yourself Safe

Although fight or flight instincts originally developed as a way to keep humans safe, in many modern-day scenarios, they do quite the opposite. Let's go back to the example from the beginning of the chapter about the chain of events in a typical chaotic day. If you wake up late in the morning and rush to make your coffee, not paying attention to what you are doing, you run the risk of haphazardly screwing the lid on your to-go cup, then sloshing boiling hot coffee over the edge of the cup and onto yourself as you bolt out the door. Although such a scenario could simply result in a stained shirt, the inattentiveness could have a more drastic effect, such as burning yourself or someone else. Driving to work in a state of panic over running late causes you to be more likely to break the rules of the road—driving too fast, making dangerous decisions when changing lanes, taking turns too fast, running yellow lights just before they turn red, etc. Additionally, the panicked state can lead to anger with yourself or others on the road, which can further impair judgment and put you at greater risk of an accident. Attempting to have a conversation with your boss if you are in fight or flight mode could result in being overly emotional and saying or doing something extreme which could place you at odds within your workplace, potentially even costing your position. Going throughout your day in a frenzy causes you to be less aware of what is going on around you, which can lead to further threats to safety like leaving a burner on, forgetting to eat or drink enough water, or neglecting those in your care (such as pets or children) as a result of your own inner distractions. Finally, as stress from the day carries into the home at the end of the day, it can pose a major threat to relationships. The more stressed out and less clear thinking you are, the more likely you are to say or do something threatening to your partner, to put yourself in an aggressive and volatile situation, and to make brash decisions that have the potential to haunt your future.

Improving Relationships

Just as we must give ourselves space to learn, grow, and process our experiences, we must give that space to those around us as well. When a partner or friend is acting in a way we don't enjoy, mindfulness can allow us to take a step back and look at the situation from a position of empathy. We can allow ourselves to hold space for whatever that person may be going through individually and express our support while also maintaining boundaries and staying in control of what we can. Everyone is deserving of space to be listened to, understood, and supported for who they are. However, it is incredibly difficult to give that space to anyone if it has not been cleared within oneself.

When we operate out of a mindless state, there is hardly any space to meet our own needs and process our own experience, much less to provide that to other people. This can lead us to be closed off to the ones we love, push them away, or act out in anger, selfishness, or aggression. If we have not given space to what is going on within us, we cannot offer full empathy to others. Only 20% of the population is recorded to practice true empathy, which can be linked to the rarity of true mindfulness among adults. Mindfulness allows us to be more present to our own needs in order to hold adequate space for the needs of others as well.

Attention and mutual respect are core elements of every functional relationship. Practicing mindfulness can improve relationships with all the people in our lives by preparing us for every engagement and calming our minds enough to be fully present in the moments we share with others. Mindfulness clears the space for us to listen intentionally to other people and pay more attention to what kind of people they are and what kind of support they need. It allows us to love other people better by increasing our awareness of how they feel most loved. By being present in the moment at hand, as opposed to trapped in the past or future, you are more likely to remember to pick up the phone and give your grandmother a call, to be fully engaged when interacting with your child, or to remember the kind of kombucha your significant other likes best from the store. Not only does mindfulness allow for more meaningful conversations and joyful memories, but it also increases the functionality of our relationships overall so that both ourselves and those we love are feeling fully respected, listened to, and encouraged.

Fostering True Joy

We often hear the term "childlike joy" to describe moments of pure bliss, enthusiasm, and full satisfaction. As people grow into adults, such moments tend to be few and far between, with many remembering the most joyful moments to have been those that occurred in childhood. The expectations of daily life become too much, and most people find themselves trapped in a cycle of constant anticipation. People spend so much time thinking about where they would rather be (on vacation, in bed, enjoying the weekend) that the days melt into each other without us realizing all the moments of our lives we are missing. The biggest societal misconception is that true happiness lies in what we do not yet have. We are flooded with lies such as "Once I can buy this new TV, then I'll be happy," or, "Once I have a partner, then I'll be happy," or, "I'll be happy once I can say I've been to five different countries." Mindfulness abolishes these lies by proving to us that the capacity for true joy lies not in the future but in the here and now. Wherever you are right now, whatever you have, and whichever stage of life you're in, mindfulness reminds you that *this* is your chance to experience beauty and satisfaction like never before. Take time to look at the flowers you did not notice growing in front of your neighbor's house, the complexity of coffee's flavor as it slides down your throat, the way your loved one's eyes crinkle when they smile, the laughter of a child, every intricate flavor of dinner, or the unique people wandering up and down the streets you drive every day to work. It is here that joy resides; all you have to do is be present enough to recognize it.

Chapter 3: Moving Mindfully in Daily Life

Coming to the Present Moment: Daily Guided Mindfulness Meditation With Journaling (Week 1)

Cultivating Mindfulness

This meditation should be done in a space where you feel fully comfortable, safe, and relaxed. Perhaps it is in a corner of your bedroom, in a garden, by your favorite lake, or even in your car. Make sure you can fully relax and avoid distractions. Some people meditate best with instrumental music or nature sounds in the background, while others prefer silence. Feel free to try multiple methods and see which is most soothing to you (this can vary depending on the day). You may do this meditation sitting in a chair, on a mat, or lying flat on your back with your palms up to the sky. You will need to give yourself 5-20 minutes of time to practice, depending on your skill level and current state. If you like, you can set a timer.

Start by coming into the moment with a few deep breaths. Settle into your body and take note of any sensations you feel. If you feel pain, tingling, warmth, or tightness in any part of your body, focus your breath into that space. Imagine any tension unfurling into openness. Notice as your thoughts arise. Take notice of them, then allow them to pass as you come back to the breath. If it is helpful, you can try a breathing pattern in order to culminate focus. To do the 4-4-4 breathing pattern, breathe in for 4 counts, hold for 4 counts, and breathe out for 4 counts. To do the 5-5-7 breathing pattern, breath in for 5 counts, hold for 5 counts, release for 7 counts. Sometimes it helps to imagine breathing in the things you wish to see more of in your daily life (creativity, love, patience, openness) and exhale the negative things (fear, negativity, sadness, stress). Allow yourself to spend a few moments in a more active state of breathing in, releasing, and paying attention to your body.

With practice, you may enter a state where your thoughts slow and you become fully grounded in the present moment. In this state, you are no longer bombarded with thoughts, nor distracted by elements of your environment. It becomes easier to return to the breath. All restlessness and tension in the body seem to melt away, and the mind reaches a flowing, liquified state. There may be days when you cannot enter into this state, and you remain restless throughout the course of the meditation. If this happens, allow it to be that way, observing every thought that arises, then letting it go.

After the time is up, begin to arrive in the moment by moving your body slightly—wiggling your fingers and toes, tensing and releasing your muscles, etc. Next, you're your eyes. Notice how bright and clear the world looks to mindful eyes. Notice the calm, transcendent feeling in your body, and continue to move with it as you go about your day.

Mindfulness Meditation Journal Prompt (Week 1):

What did you feel in your body before beginning? What do you feel now?

Which thoughts continued to arise in your consciousness? Could these thoughts have been trying to teach you something or speak to a deeper need you may have?

How does the world look after opening your eyes? What do you notice?

Come back after going about your day for several hours. Did you bring mindfulness with you into the world? If so, how?

Coming to the Present Moment: Daily Guided Mindfulness Meditation With Journaling (Week 2)

Taking Mindfulness Into the World

This meditation will be done with your eyes open in moments if your daily life. This is not a specific meditation you have to set aside time for, but rather a state you come into. Notice where your attention goes in a given moment. If your attention is drawn to a particular sight, like the nearest tree or a view from the top of a mountain, allow yourself to see it fully. Repeatedly tell yourself, "see, see, see." Breathe as you allow your eyes to truly become totally focused and take in the image fully, allowing it to become a part of your awareness.

If your attention is drawn to an auditory experience, such as the sound of cars on a city street, a rushing body of water, or an internal monologue, give full attention to that thing. Soak in that auditory experience, breathing slowly and telling yourself, "hear, hear, hear."

You may also be drawn to a particular physical or emotional experience within the body. This experience may be positive, like a pleasant bodily sensation or a feeling of joy. It may also be negative, like physical pain, or feelings of anger or feel. Either way, allow yourself to become fully present with what is there, breathing into the experience and seeing what it has to teach you. Breathe into that bodily experience, telling yourself, "feel, feel, feel."

Throughout the day, you'll find that your attention is pulled in various directions. Mindfulness is the choice to tune in to whichever place you're going in a given moment and give full attention to that experience for whatever it is.

Mindfulness Meditation Journal Prompt (Week 2):

How difficult was it to bring mindfulness into your daily life in this way? Where did you face the most challenges?

Did your attention tend towards certain experiences (visual, auditory, bodily) more than others?

Describe a specific moment where you brought mindfulness to your experience and felt truly present. What did you observe?

Coming to the Present Moment: Daily Guided Mindfulness Meditation With Journaling (Week 3)

Mindfulness at Work (or School)

The first part of this meditation should happen in a place outside of work, where you feel safe, calm, and separated from the issues you may face in the workplace. Start by identifying your biggest struggles at work. The journal portion will give you a space to write them down. Do you struggle with productivity? Boredom? Stress? Conflict resolution? Work relationships? Once you have identified your most significant area(s) of struggle, close your eyes and visualize what that unpleasant experience looks like. Perhaps it looks like you, rushing around mindlessly like a bee in a hive, stressed out and too overbooked to step away and breathe because there are more calls to make, more e-mails to send, more things to do. Or, perhaps it is the co-worker, professor, or boss that makes your stomach drop whenever you think about having to interact with them. Perhaps you feel unfulfilled at work and find yourself constantly checking the clock, thinking about the moment you get to leave. Maybe you have so many things to do and no idea where to start, so you waste a lot of time on mindless tasks. Whatever your struggles at work are, use your time and space away from work to safely visualize the situation. Breathe into the mental circumstance.

As you breathe, begin to envision what this experience would look like if it went the way you want it to. Perhaps it looks like the mental clarity that allows you to know exactly what needs to get done and how to make the best possible use of your time. It could be a greater sense of calm and courage when talking with your difficult boss or co-worker and having your message be well-received on their end. It may also be a deeper sense of satisfaction and enjoyment in the work you're doing, providing you the ability to step back and feel a sense of joy with where you're at, without constantly thinking about the next thing. Reframe the moment in your mind until you've created a mental space that feels good. Let yourself sit there, breathing, soaking it in for several minutes.

Once you go into the workplace (or school), you can bring this meditation into your life by going back to the peaceful mental image you've created over and over again. When you begin to feel stressed, bored, anxious, or unproductive, return to the space where you do not feel those things. Bring that energy into your daily work life, and watch how it revolutionizes your experience.

Mindfulness Meditation Journal Prompt (Week 3):

What do you identify as your biggest challenge(s) at work or school?

How does it look when you reframe your struggles to create a positive mental image?

What do you observe about bringing this positive mental image into difficult situations in the workplace or at school?

Mini Meditation Toolbox: 15 Quick and Easy Meditations to Integrate Mindfulness Into Your Daily Life

One-Minute Mindfulness
- Find a space where you can be alone, like on your bathroom break or in your car right before going into work, school, or home at the end of the day.
- Set a timer for one minute
- Close your eyes and focus exclusively on your breathing
- Take notice of the stresses, thoughts, and anxieties that arise, then let them go
- When you open your eyes, notice how you feel de-stressed, clear-minded, and prepared to go about your upcoming tasks and interactions with others

5-Minute Body Scan
- Set a timer for 5 minutes (if needed)
- Close your eyes and take several deep, cleansing breaths. You may use the 4-4-4 or 5-5-7 breathing patterns to deepen the breath
- Begin to bring attention to your body
- Take notice of any sensations that arise-- warmth, tingling, tension, etc.
- Bring your attention to the soles of the feet. Tighten your muscles by curling your toes, then release. What sensations do you feel?

- Continue moving up the body to your calves, hips, abdomen, chest, hands, arms, face, and neck. Observe any sensations that arise, and breathe into those sensations.
- Tighten and release the muscles in each of these areas, allowing any pent-up energy or resistance to be released
- Feel your body become grounded, relaxing completely into the floor, bed, or chair as you come into the present moment in your body and all tension melts away

Mindful Bath/Shower (10-minute meditation)
- As you begin your bath or shower, take a moment to breathe. Remove yourself from the stresses of the day and allow yourself to re-center
- Bring attention to each part of your body as you wash it
- Take notice of any sensations you feel as you move from the soles of your feet to the ends of your hair
- Breathe in the pleasant scent of the soaps and the warmth of the water. Allow yourself to feel clean, warm, and safe.
- As you wash each part of your body, thank it for what it does for you. Then, thank yourself for taking care of your body.

Mindful Morning Routine (15-30 minutes)

- Before getting out of bed, begin to stretch gently, letting thoughts come and go as your mind and body wake up. Do not rush yourself.
- Once you are ready to get out of bed, bring your attention to the space around you and the day ahead. Feel yourself become fully present in that space and prepared to move mindfully through your day
- Pay attention to every move you make, from putting on clothes, to washing your face, to setting the water on the stove to boil.
- Cultivate your awareness for the day ahead by moving slowly and calmly, one task at a time, becoming fully awake to the world

Mindful Housekeeping
- Allow yourself to become focused on the task at hand and only that task. Let every other thing you have to do or think about fade into the background.
- Bring your attention to the breath and the specific way your body moves as you complete a particular task or chore
- Give space to any thoughts or emotions that arise in your consciousness, allowing yourself to process them in a mindful state

Mindful Sit-and-Drink (10-minute meditation)

- Find a calm, quiet space where you can sit and observe the world around you (preferably outside or near a window looking outside)
- Pour a glass of your favorite tea, coffee, or cocktail to enjoy
- Eliminate all distractions. Draw your attention to the intricate flavors of the drink, and the pleasure of pulling something you enjoy into your body
- Take notice of the things happening around you. Find the things in the environment that bring you the most peace, and allow their presence with you to help you calm your mind. Become completely indulged in the moment.

Mindful Scheduling (10-minute meditation)

- Sit down with a pen and paper and center yourself with five deep breaths.
- Think about the days to come. Consider your priorities, remembering that every task is significant and an opportunity for increased mindfulness
- Ask yourself, "Am I giving myself adequate time to bring mindfulness and intentionality into each of these activities?"
- Take notice of any activities you feel you won't be able to be fully present for. Consider taking a thing or two off the list and saving them for a better time.
- Take notice of any feelings of stress, nervousness, or rush you feel in regards to your schedule. Breathe into those feelings.

- As you continue to write your schedule, allow yourself to feel empowered, in control, and prepared to be mindful of everything you are about to do

Mindful Driving

- Leave the house with plenty of time to be relaxed and focused. After entering the car, take a few moments to breathe and center yourself
- Once you start to drive, begin to take note of the things passing by. What do you see today that you did not see yesterday?
- Breathe in your visual surroundings, using them to center and remind yourself: "I am here. I am in this community. This is my life, and I am awake to it."

Mindful Walking (10-20-minute meditation)

- Choose an area where you can relax and bring attention to your surroundings. This can be in a park, in the city, on the beach, in your neighborhood, etc.
- Set out on your walk with no distractions
- Take notice of the things your eyes fall upon. If something specific catches your attention, allow yourself to pause and breathe it in.
- Pay attention to the sounds that surround you, giving yourself space to truly hear them

- Pay attention to the feeling of your feet on the pavement, the swing of your arms at your sides, and the rhythm of your breath
- Let your heart expand in curiosity and openness to whatever is ready to meet you in this space
- Allow yourself to become totally saturated with your surroundings, remembering that everything you see, hear, and feel is a part of you

Mindful Cooking and Eating

- As you enter the kitchen to prepare food, take a moment to center yourself in the moment with a few deep breaths
- Give every moment of the cooking process your full attention, from washing, to cutting, to cooking. Become fully immersed in the process (you can do this even with simple meals, like mindfully spreading peanut butter on bread)
- Breathe loving-kindness into the cooking process, remembering that the food you make will provide nourishment to yourself and others
- Once the food is ready, clear the eating space of distractions. Avoid multi tasking
- Chew every bite of food 20-30 times, letting yourself be engulfed in the flavor and practicing gratitude for the nourishment
- Walk away from your meal feeling truly nourished and renewed

Mindful Waiting
- The next time you're trying to distract yourself at the doctor's office, the mechanic, or waiting for a friend or colleague to arrive, remind yourself that waiting is one of the most sacred times to engage in mindfulness
- Breathe into the moment, becoming aware of what surrounds you
- Bring awareness to your body. How are you feeling? Take note of any sensations
- Become aware of the thoughts that come once you stop numbing yourself with distractions. What things are running through your mind?
- Pay attention to the deeper thoughts you may have previously been ignoring. Ask yourself what you can learn about yourself and your life, or if there are any actions you need to take.

Mindful Creativity (at least 5 minutes)
- Set aside anywhere from five minutes to several hours of undivided time
- Engage in a creative project like art, writing, dancing, etc.
- Bring full presence to the creative project and try to eliminate all expectations. Allow the moment to carry you.
- Pay attention to how your mind and body react as the moment carries you. How do you feel?
- Examine what you create as a result of this free-flowing creativity

Mindful Play
- Dedicate time each week to doing something truly fun—something that makes you feel like a kid again (climbing a tree, swimming in the lake, drawing with chalk, baking cookies, having a game night, etc.)
- Eliminate all distractions and allow this to be a moment to step away from your everyday life and responsibilities
- Allow yourself to become lost in the childlike joy of play. Laugh loudly, let your body dance, be curious.
- Let the feeling of childlike joy saturate your body and carry this joy with you as you move back into your daily life.

Mindful Movement (10-30 minutes)
- Choose one of your favorite forms of movement (swimming, walking, dancing, going to the gym, etc.) and dedicate at least ten minutes to it
- As you begin to move, establish a deeper sense of body awareness. Pay attention to the feelings in your body as you begin to warm up and exercise
- Pay attention to the way your heart beats, your lungs heave, your face begins to sweat, and your body tingles with the sense of being alive
- Thank your body for all it does for you.

Mindful Listening/Quality Time

- Apply this meditation to any quality time you spend with another person, whether that is grabbing coffee or going for a walk with a loved one, interacting with co-workers, are conversing with the grocery store cashier
- Before interacting with others, bring attention to your levels of empathy. Set the intention to hold space for other people and the moments you share with them
- Eliminate distractions (like technology) and allow yourself to put everything else going on in your life on pause in order to be fully present
- One of the best ways to show love for people and to cultivate personal mindfulness is through mindful listening. Focus all of your attention on the other person and what they are saying. When you ask how their day is going, be present to hear the answer.
- Do not think of what your next move will be, what you will say, or where you will go. Simply be there, showing loving-kindness, holding space, and taking it all in.

Mini Meditation Toolbox: 10 Quick and Easy Meditations to Ease Stress, Depression, Addiction, Anxiety, Pain, Distraction, and Loss Using Mindfulness

Journaling the Consciousness (10-minute meditation)
- Sit down with a journal and a pen and set your timer for 10 minutes
- As thoughts, worries, or emotions arise, immediately write them down. Do not worry about structure, grammar, or content, just write.
- When the time is up, look over what you wrote
- Ask yourself which themes seem to reoccur. Where are you feeling stress in your life? What is occupying most of your mental space?
- Close your eyes and take a few moments to breathe and meditate on the thing(s) that need your attention the most
- Open your eyes. Notice how you feel lighter and in touch with your experience

Distraction Cleanse: Clearing the Space in your Mind
- *Find a quiet place and begin to breathe*
- Ask yourself: "What is distracting me from being present right now?"
- Give space to that distraction, whether it is an invasive thought, personal emotion, or someone else's emotion

- Say to yourself: "I am letting my distractions move through me as I ground myself in the present moment. Nothing is more important than right now."
- Breathe until you feel the distraction melt away into presence and mental clarity.

Re-Writing the Moment: A Short Meditation to Ease Emotional Pain of the Past
- Sit down with a journal and a pen and set your timer for 1 minute
- Take this 1 minute to write down any moment(s) of the past which have caused you a lot of pain
- After the minute is up, choose one of the painful moments, close your eyes, and begin to imagine the moment in a safe way. Be sure to keep breathing.
- When you open your eyes, take your pen and paper and re-imagine the painful moment. What do you wish had happened? How do you wish you could think about the moment now?
- After re-imagining the painful moment, remind yourself that this is a new moment. Everyone has painful memories, but you do not have to stay in spaces of the past, which are painful for you.
- Close your eyes, take a few more breaths, and say to yourself, "I release the pain of that moment of the past. This is a new moment, and I will move with it."

Re-claiming your Inner Power: A Short Meditation to Face Addiction

- Breathe into the moment, allowing yourself to think about the implications your addiction has on your life
- Without judgment, question your addiction. Ask yourself, "What has been left empty in me that I am trying to fill with this?" Listen for any emotions or past experiences of trauma, grief, or abandonment that arise. Allow them to be there.
- Say to yourself, "Now that I understand the root of my addiction, I can begin to be set free."
- With closed eyes, begin to breathe. With each breath, imagine your addiction's hold on you weakening and weakening until eventually, you have been released.
- Move forward into your life with the idea that your addiction's hold on you is loosening, day by day.

Letter to the Lost: A Short Meditation to Address Grief and Loss

- Sit down with a journal and a pen and take five deep breaths to bring you into the moment
- Allow someone you have lost to come to mind. This can be a relationship that has ended, someone who has died, etc.
- Close your eyes and breathe into the space this person has left empty within you. Allow yourself to experience any emotions that arise.
- When you open your eyes, take a few minutes to write what you wish you could have said to that person

- After you have finished your letter, close your eyes again. Tell your grief that it is okay for it to be there. With every breath, imagine yourself moving forward in your life, released from every regret you may have with someone you've lost

In with The Positive, Out with the Negative: A Short Breathing Technique
- Find a comfortable space and prepare to use the 5-5-7 breathing technique
- Breathe in for five counts and think of something positive you want to bring into this moment (kindness, peace, wisdom, etc.)
- Hold for five counts, allowing this positive thing to fill your body
- Exhale for seven counts, thinking of something negative you want to release from your body in this moment (stress, tension, selfishness, etc.)
- Begin again with a second emotion. Do this as many times as you like until you feel well-equipped with positive emotions and have released all negative ones

Space to Breathe: A Short Meditation to Gain Control over your Anxiety
- When you begin to feel anxious, step away, take a breath, and ground yourself in the moment by finding one thing you can see, one thing you can hear, and one thing you can feel. Focus deeply on each thing.

- Allow your anxiety space to exist. Remember, anxiety is the reaction your emotional brain has when it senses a threat. You can bring yourself back from catastrophe mode by using the rational brain to repeatedly remind yourself: "I am safe. I am in control. I am capable of being calm."
- Keep breathing and saying these rational-brained affirmations until you begin to feel your anxiety melt away
- Move into the next moment feeling calm, anxiety-free, and empowered

Emotion Coding: A Short Meditation to Bring you in Touch with your Emotions

- Find a quiet, comfortable place where you can easily connect with yourself
- Close your eyes and breathe deeply (you may use a breathing pattern if desired)
- Begin to travel inwards. Say to yourself, "I am ready to accept the emotions that are here."
- Wait patiently, focusing on the breath, and observing every emotion that rises to the surface.
- When an emotion arises, ask yourself a series of questions:

    1. "Is this emotion mine or someone else's?"
    2. "Does this emotion serve me or hold me back?"
    3. "What is this emotion trying to teach me?"
    4. "Should I release this emotion or put it into action?"

- When it comes to answering each question, listen to your intuition. The answers to each question are already within you. Do not question your natural answers.
- If you are being told to release an old or negative emotion, or an emotion that belongs to someone else, breathe and imagine it melting away with every exhale
- If you are being told to foster a positive emotion or a strong emotion that can create positive change in the world, sit with that, breathing, and being open to how that emotion can be useful.

The "I Love…" Gratitude Meditation (2-minute meditation)

- Find a private space, preferably one in front of a mirror
- Start a timer for 2 minutes
- For two minutes, speak out loud sentences of gratitude beginning with the words "I love…" ("I love my partner," "I love coffee," "I love my cat," "I love sunflowers," I love my mom," "I love to dance," "I love that I am healthy,").
- Say as many things as you can, one after the other. Do not think too much, simply let the things you love flow from your lips
- When the timer goes off, look in the mirror and say "And I love you," to yourself
- Feel the magic of gratitude transforming your life, your self-confidence, and your ability to be mindful

The Mindful Manifestation: A Short Meditation to Manifest what you Want in Life

- Sit down with a journal and pen
- Begin to cultivate mindfulness by bringing attention to your breath and any sensations in your body
- Ask yourself the question: "What do I want most in life?"
- As the answers start to come, open your eyes and begin to write your desires with the words "I manifest…" in front of them ("I manifest empathy." "I manifest peace of mind." "I manifest protection." "I manifest safety." "I manifest love." "I manifest awareness." "I manifest wisdom." "I manifest pure joy.")
- With each manifestation, close your eyes, and say it to yourself at least three times. Feel this manifestation become a part of your reality.

PART II

Chapter 1: Energy Healing- The Key to Holistic Health

Understanding the impacts of energy imbalances and corresponding physical, mental, spiritual health

How many times have you, or another adult in your life, said the words "I just don't have the energy I used to have."? Most adults know the feeling of looking at the energy children have as they run about, enjoying life, exploring their surroundings, and never seeming to grow tired. Many of us are left reflecting back on the distant past when we, too, had such energy and wondering where it went.

From the time children enter school, they begin to be presented with expectations. Stand in a straight line, raise your hand, don't talk while the teacher is talking. Each year, the level of responsibility and expectation seems to increase. While rules, regulations, and individual responsibility are important for a functioning society, there are numerous expectations and social pressures put on people as they grow, which can be incredibly harmful.

It is generally around middle school when children become more acutely aware of their bodies and societal beauty standards, which tell them what they "should" look like. Children are likely to become aware of the trends, such as which clothes the "cool kids" are wearing. The endless battle to feel like enough begins, and can lead to a plethora of issues with self-esteem, eating disorders, and mental illness. In addition to the basic societal pressures to be accepted and considered attractive, many children are also faced with difficult situations at home where their own needs are not being met, they are having to provide for and protect themselves in the only ways they know how, avoid abusive parents, care for younger siblings, or worry about if they'll have anything to eat that day. Even if children have a relatively healthy home life, this is the age when they will begin to become aware of the issues that plague their family (every family has issues) whether this is divorce, an alcoholic parent, the death of a pet or loved one, etc.

We live in a society that thrives off of consumerism. We are flooded with images of how the next vacation, new pair of shoes, nicer car, nicer house, or perfect partner will make us happy, and all of the things we need to change about ourselves in order to fulfill those things. Eventually, all the energy we had as a child starts going towards maintaining our image in society, trying to have all the "best" life has to offer (which always happens to be everything we do not have), and attempting to be as "successful" as possible in the eyes of society and other people. With no time to rest in the present moment, recharge, and appreciate what we already have, it is no wonder, so many of us are completely drained of energy. In such a fast-paced society that discourages breaks, our energy will become depleted, and we will find ourselves thrown out of balance and unable to obtain true happiness and well-being. Over time, this depletion and imbalance can lead to a sense of spiritual disconnection, extreme mental health issues, and an increased risk of physical pain, illness, and even earlier death.

Chapter 2: Energy Healing and Overcoming Suffering

Energy and Grief/Trauma

Every human being knows that loss is a natural part of life. The one certain thing in life is that we, and everyone we know, is going to die. However, in such a fast-paced society, we are often given a very short grace period before being expected to swallow our grief and "move on" when we lose those closest to us. It is not abnormal for people to receive a bereavement period of only a few days before being expected to be back in the classroom or office and be fully functional. There is very little space for the grief journey, and most people are expected to harbor their feelings and keep their grief to themselves.

The grief process is expansive and incredibly energy draining. When we don't receive the adequate support from those around us, or adequate space to heal, our body begins to break down piece by piece. The empty spaces within us will swallow us up into states of depression, numbness, isolation, and pure exhaustion. Just like a wound being denied the correct treatment and care, the wounds of unresolved grief will fester and leave us feeling completely drained of energy and vitality for life.

Unresolved trauma also has an incredibly destructive impact on the body. Trauma can occur as a result of grief itself, as well as emotional or domestic abuse, accident or illness, war, sexual assault, childhood maltreatment, etc. The body holds trauma in various places, and the brain switches over from the logical ability to discern safety and danger into an easily triggered emotional state. An overactive emotional brain loses the ability to think clearly, make decisions, and recognize threats. People who have unresolved trauma are likely to be easily triggered and deal with unexplained outbursts of anger, fear, relationship issues, reckless behavior, and health problems. When trauma sits in the body unresolved, the brain is unable to understand that the traumatic event has ended. Therefore, it will stay in a consistent fight-or-flight state, which is incredibly draining and will leave the body with no energy. Not only will trauma victims experience low energy levels, but they will also experience severe issues maintaining positive relationships and overall well-being.

Energy and Mental Health

There are numerous factors that can contribute to mental health issues. As previously discussed, societal issues and unresolved grief and trauma can yield higher levels of anxiety, depression, and PTSD. It is also very common for people to suffer from mood disorders, personality disorders, disordered eating, substance abuse, etc. The list is long for psychological ailments and how they happen, and it has been proven that 1 in 3 people will be diagnosed with a mental illness in their lifetime. Even without a specific disorder, most people will have periods of life where their mental health suffers greatly.

No matter what a person's struggle with mental health looks like, or what they are doing (or not doing) in terms of treatment, the body expends a lot of energy when a part of it is unwell.

Daily Energy Regulation

No matter what it is in your life that is causing you to feel depleted, it is vital to pay attention to the energy fields within the body and identify the areas of greatest pain and imbalance. In the spectrum of health, people often take measures such as going to see the doctor, therapist, or grief counselor, taking medication, and making lifestyle changes such as finding a hobby or increasing exercise. However, a piece that is commonly overlooked in the healing journey is healing energetically. No matter how much you invest in your mental, physical, emotional, and spiritual health, if your energies remain imbalanced, it is impossible to reach a state of full wellness. That being said, energy healing is the missing piece in most people's quests for holistic health.

In many cases, it can be beneficial to seek the help of energy healers, massage therapists, and reiki, craniosacral therapy, or bodywork practitioners. These practitioners are trained in getting in touch with your energy centers and helping bring them back into balance through healing touch, body movements, and visualization techniques. If you are dealing with energy imbalance, seeing a practitioner can be an excellent investment in unlocking your highest levels of health and joy in life.

It is also possible to use a variation of the body scan mediation from chapter 3 to check in with your energy levels on your own. By taking notice of the sensations in each area of your body, you can come closer in touch with any area of your body where you experience regular pain, tension, or other unpleasant feelings. This is often a sign of imbalance or trapped energy. Additionally, the tense and release technique in each area of the body can yield healing and balance by releasing negative energy and tension. It is important to check in with yourself daily, asking your body where energy may be trapped or depleted and what you can do to replenish yourself.

Chapter 3: The Daily Energy Healing Journey

Understanding Your Energy Field: Daily Energy Healing Meditation with Journaling (Week 5)

There is a great variety when it comes to human energy fields. People experience varying levels of sensitivity to the energy of other people and the environment. Some people are incredibly in tune with "vibes"; others are empaths who feel the emotional experiences of others on a deep level, while still others experience very little of either. There is also a lot of variation in the way people recharge energetically, as well as what depletes them. In the common case of introverts and extroverts, for example, introverts need time alone to replenish their energy and feel balanced, while extroverts recharge in stimulating environments with other people around. One of the first steps to protecting your personal energetic field is to understand how it works.

Understanding Your Energy Field Journal Prompt (Week 5):

When you feel exhausted and not like yourself, which activities are most likely to replenish your energy? Do you enjoy a night out with friends? Yoga? A walk in the park? Leisure reading? Finding a new adventure? Taking a bubble bath? Listening to your favorite music on blast? List 5-10 activities that help you gain balance and feel energized.

Now, make a list of the things that make you feel most drained. These can be large things, like a specific task at your job, or small things like doing the dishes. You may find that you feel drained if you spend too much time alone or, consequently, when you spend too much time around other people.

When it comes to activities that make you feel drained, ask yourself to what extent that specific thing is necessary in your life. If you find yourself feeling drained from spending too much time around other people, for example, you can easily make a change by scheduling more "nothing time" or "alone time" into your days and taking the time you need to replenish. Household tasks and daily responsibilities are necessary, but by being aware of the ones that drain you the most, you can bring more attention to the process and doing what you need to replenish energy before or after.

Protecting Your Energy Field: Daily Energy Healing Meditation with Journaling (Week 6)

Close your eyes and ask yourself, "what does my energy field look like?" Write down any specific colors, textures, shapes, or patterns of movement.

Once you have an image in your mind of your energy field, ask yourself, "What does it look like for outside energies to enter my field?" Write down what healthy and unhealthy outside energies look like.

Then ask yourself, "How can I regulate the energies entering my field? What does it look like when I decide what I will let in?" Describe this process.

Finally, ask yourself, "How does my body feel when I regulate what I allow to enter my energy field?" Write down everything that comes to mind.

Healing Through Trapped Emotion Release: Daily Energy Healing Meditation with Journaling (Week 7)

In our society, we are often faced with life circumstances that force us to repress our basic human emotions. It is very possible for anger, rage, or grief to become stuck in the body because it is considered "impractical" to have those reactions in public. Similarly, we often hear about people being described as "annoyingly happy" or "overly emotional." Most of us are taught not only to manage our emotions but to distance ourselves from them and react emotionally only in certain contexts. Additionally, we tend to suppress negative emotions such as fear, shame, inadequacy, and insecurity, for the purpose of appearing like we have everything together. Between life events and societal expectations, it is very easy for the emotions we suppress to become trapped in our bodies, which can create adverse health effects, negatively impact our relationships, and keep us from living our best lives.

Begin by making a list of as many emotions as you can think of

Run down the list of emotions one by one, asking yourself, "Is there anywhere in my body I am holding *particular emotion*?"

Write down the emotions you feel are trapped. Take some time to journal about how certain emotions arose, or times when you felt you had to suppress your emotions.

With each emotion you have labeled as being trapped, write: "I give myself permission to release this *particular emotion*

Cultivating Self-Trust in your Healing Journey: Daily Energy Healing Meditation With Journaling (Week 8)

No matter what you do in your life, there will always be people who don't understand the choices you make, or who judge the path you are on. When it comes to renewing and protecting your energy, there is no room for anyone else's opinions or emotions in regards to your journey. It requires a great deal of self-trust to go your own way and let what other people think about it roll off your back. For this reason, it is vital to begin everyday establishing a sense of self-trust with your own journey and energy management skills. The following four journal questions will help you direct your energy before going about your day.

What are you most grateful for today?

What are your intentions for how you will direct your energy today?

What are your fears/things you perceive as a potential threat?

What are your commitments to yourself and the world?

Mini Meditation Toolbox: 25 Quick and Easy Energy Restoration and Protection Meditations

One-Minute Energy Cleanse

- This meditation is useful if you find yourself with a person or in a specific situation that feels negative or energetically draining. You do not need to be alone to complete this meditation
- Pause where you are and allow yourself to take a few deep, cleansing breaths
- Focus exclusively on your breathing; you may close your eyes or leave them open
- Feel the inner power within the core of your body, around your abdomen. Remind yourself that you are in control and have the power to maintain balance.
- As you inhale, pull love, light, and peace into your body
- As you exhale, breathe out pain, annoyance, and toxicity

Energy from the Earth

- Begin by entering a space in nature. This can be on the beach, in the mountains, near a river, in a garden, by the lake, or in your own yard
- If possible, slip your shoes off, so your bare feet are in contact with the earth

- Start with a few cleansing breaths, taking note of everything you see, hear, smell, and feel in your environment
- Placing the soles of your feet on the ground, begin to breathe, pulling the energy from the earth up through your body
- Remember that you are One with the nature that courses around you. Allow it to heal what is broken within you and leave you feeling rejuvenated

Re-Centering Head Hold (3-5 minute meditation)
- Close your eyes and place the palm of one hand horizontally across the crown of your head, and the other palm across your forehead (over the energetic points of the Crown and Third Eye chakras). This position can be done while standing, sitting, or lying down.
- While clutching your head in this position, bring attention to any sensations in your body. What needs your attention most right now?
- Allow yourself to come back to the present moment, feeling grounded in your body and in your experience
- Breathe in awareness, focus, and comfort, exhaling anxiety and distraction
- When you open your eyes, notice how you feel grounded in your space

The Cloak of Protection

- This meditation is useful for energy protection before going out into the world, whether that is to work, the supermarket, an appointment, etc.
- Although you do not know what kinds of energies you may encounter, or which people may try to take your energy from you, remind yourself that you are in control of your own energy and that you have the capacity to protect yourself
- Close your eyes and imagine a dark-blue, almost black cloak made of a soft, thick material like a velvet night sky. The cloak is full-length with a hood to protect all of your chakras.
- Imagine a ray of light outlining the cloak in whatever color(s) feel most magical, protective, and authentic to who you are
- Set off into the world knowing that you are safe within yourself and your energy cloak and that you do not need to be afraid

De-Cluttering your Space

- When energy is lacking or out of balance, the spaces we live in are likely to reflect that imbalance with clutter and messiness. The more we feel like we "don't have our lives together," the more likely we are to have a messy desk, dishes piling up in the sink, laundry that still needs to be folded, or a car that has not been cleared of trash
- Such spaces do not allow for peace and mental clarity and can be even more draining to come back to after a long day

- Dedicate yourself to one area of your life to de-clutter. This can be your kitchen, your car, your bedroom, etc. Close your eyes before beginning and take a few deep, cleansing breaths to approach the task calmly
- Begin to address all of the clutter in the space, not only picking it up but putting it into a designated area where it can be organized and easy to find
- You may find that you want to create a special shelf or move some furniture around to make the space less cluttered. As you go, notice the energy that continues to unfold in your body
- When you finish, place a "clutter basket" in your room, the car, the living room, etc. where you can compile all the clutter throughout the day and put it away before bed

De-Cluttering your Mind (5-minute meditation)
- Close your eyes and begin to breathe deeply
- Ask yourself, "What is taking up the most space in my mind right now?"
- Bring your attention to whatever it is that is distracting you, and why it makes you feel out of control
- Breathe into that situation, saying, "I have control over this situation, and I am not going to let it spill out into the rest of my day. I am clearing this space."

The Energy-Ownership Mantra

- This meditation is ideal to perform in the morning, or before going out to interact with the world or other people
- Sit in a place where you feel energized (on the porch, in your meditation corner, etc.)
- Close your eyes and begin to breathe, checking in with any unresolved emotions or senses within the body
- Now begin to picture your energy field. Say to yourself: "My energy field is my sacred space, and other energies will only permeate it when I allow them to."
- Breathe into this thought for several moments
- Now, bring this thought into your mental space: "I have the wisdom to discern what belongs to me and what belongs to other people. I can be empathetic and attentive to other people's emotions, struggles, and opinions without assuming responsibility for them."

Epsom Bath Energy Renewal
- Begin by selecting your favorite scented Epsom salts. You may also customize your bath with petals, oils, and candles as according to the healing plants, herbs, and oils listed in Chapter 4
- Run a hot bath, letting your Epsom salts and other elements saturate the water
- Customize your space with the light of candles, meditative music, and anything else that makes you feel at peace

- Find a comfortable position inside the tub. Close your eyes, and feel your entire body relax into the heat and gentle movement of the water.
- Begin to conduct a body scan, feeling entirely vulnerable to this moment at peace with only yourself
- Ask your body, "What do I need right now?"
- The water should be hot enough that you begin to sweat (be sure to have a glass of water nearby). As you sweat, imagine your body purging itself of every blockage, every impurity, and every negativity

Sealing your Energy Field

- Close your eyes and begin to breathe
- Bring the image of your energy field to your mind. You may picture a wall, a bubble, or a glowing ring of light (this image may also differ depending on the day)
- Picture what other energies look like, floating around your field like particles in an atom. Say to yourself, "I am in control of what comes in."
- Imagine yourself recognizing people who are trying to take your energy or bear their burdens. Imagine any fear, anger, or resentment you may feel.

- Say to yourself, "No, not today." Imagine your bubble becoming impermeable, your wall being sealed, your glowing ring of light rejecting anything that does not belong inside
- Allow yourself to feel empowered over your energy, without feeling any resentment or judgment towards those who once posed a threat

Building your Sanctuary
- Sit down and close your eyes, beginning to breathe into yourself
- With each breath, ask yourself, "What makes me feel safe?" Repeat three times.
- Switch the phrase to "What makes me feel at peace?" Repeat three times.
- Switch the phrase to "What makes me feel loving?" Repeat three times
- Switch to "What makes me feel joy?"
- Lastly, ask yourself, "What makes me feel renewed?"
- When you ask yourself these questions, you may see certain crystals, scenes in nature, types of music, plants, aromas, decorations, activities, or color schemes. Take note of whatever comes to mind.
- Use these things that come to you in meditation to mindfully cultivate a space for yourself to come into every day when you need time to recharge. This can be a meditation corner, a spot in the

backyard, or any other space that is sacred to you and provides feelings of security and rest.

Cultivating Non-Reaction

- This meditation can be used when encountering a stressful situation, having a difficult conversation, or otherwise entering a state of nervous or angry energy
- Before responding to whatever the negative stimulant is, breathe into the moment. Close your eyes if needed.
- Tell yourself, "I can choose not to expend energy on this interaction. I can choose to move peacefully into the next moment."
- Feel the tension within you melt away as you make the choice not to internalize the stress of the situation or the negative energy coming at you

Boundary Setting

- Find a quiet place to sit and self-reflect. Breathe into the moment
- After you have settled into your breath, ask yourself, "What people, circumstances, or tasks drain my energy and leave me feeling agitated or exhausted?"
- Allow the answers to rise into your consciousness at will. Meditate on every name, every task, every circumstance which makes you feel tense and throws your energy out of balance.

- With each name, circumstance, and task, say to yourself, "This *person, place, thing* has no power over me. I can maintain my energy in spite of it."
- Next, ask yourself, "Where do I need to draw the line with this *person, place, thing*?"
- Listen to your intuition tell you what your boundaries should be. Perhaps, this looks like gently cutting off a toxic person, or limiting your interaction time with them. It could be quitting a job that is no longer good for you or asking for accommodations to make your environment more positive. It could be telling someone who expects you to bear their burdens that their energies are no longer your responsibility. Or, perhaps it is to establish a self-care activity to do directly after a draining task.

Trigger Awareness
- If your energy has ever been thrown out of balance by trauma, there are likely still factors of your environment that can strike at any time, causing your body to react in the same way it did at the time of the trauma.
- Breathe into the moment, asking yourself, "what elements of my environment cause me to lose control of my logic and feel afraid, helpless, irrational, in pain, or otherwise unbalanced or unhealthy energetically."
- These elements are called "triggers." Bring your awareness to these triggers, simply allowing them to be there without judgment.

- Say to yourself, "that moment in time is over. I can now release myself."

Energetic Tapping
- Begin by determining 3-5 affirmations or manifestations for the day ahead ("I manifest peace," "I am content," "I am present," "I manifest energy," "I am growing," "I manifest healing," "I manifest loving-kindness," etc.)
- Breathe deeply, pondering the affirmations/manifestations
- Choose your first manifestation/affirmation. With your index and middle fingers on both hands, begin tapping lightly on the crown of your head, repeating the manifestation or affirmation three times
- Move to the temples, tapping and saying the manifestation/affirmation three times
- Repeat at the inner corners of the brow bone
- Repeat just above the brow line
- Repeat at the top of the cheekbones
- Repeat below the ear lobes at the crest of the jawbone
- Repeat at the top of the chest
- Repeat on the left wrist, then switch to the right wrist
- Switch to the next affirmation/manifestation and go through the process again, staying in touch with your breath throughout

Listening to your Intuition

- Find a space where you feel completely comfortable and relaxed
- Begin to breathe deeply, coming into the present moment
- Ask yourself, "What does my inner self need me to know right now?"
- Keep breathing, holding space for whatever answer arises
- If necessary, you can ask follow-up questions to yourself, like "Is there any threat I need to be prepared to protect myself from?" or "How can I best love the world today?" Or "What do I need to do to take care of myself today?"
- Continue to breathe and hold space, trusting that your heart will guide you to make the correct decisions for yourself

Memory Reclamation (specifically for healing of trauma victims)

- Find a space where you feel totally safe and undisturbed. It is best to do this meditation on a day where you can invest in self care and rest.
- Begin to breathe, telling yourself, "I am safe. I am safe. I am safe."
- Allow the memory of a particularly traumatic event to come to your mind. Continue to breathe, telling yourself, "I am safe."

- Pay attention to the details of that memory. What do you see? What do you hear? What do you feel?
- As the memory progresses, allow it to release its energetic hold on your body. Tell yourself, "That was then. This is now. I am safe."
- Feel the trauma release its hold on you, restoring itself to a basic memory of the past

Defining your Needs

- Sit in a peaceful place, breathing into the moment
- Bring attention to any pain or unrest within your body. Without judgment, allow it to be there, asking if there is anything you should learn from it.
- Generally, where there is pain or unrest, there is a need being left unmet. Ask yourself, "What is it that I need?"
- Allow your needs to arise into your consciousness ("I need a day off for my mental health," "I need a trip into nature," "I need a bath," "I need a warm, nourishing meal," "I need to go to sleep early," etc.)
- Breathe into each need, envisioning yourself meeting that particular need
- Ask yourself, "Is there anyone else I need to make aware of these needs?"
- Envision yourself having a calm conversation about your needs with your boss, your partner, your family, or a friend. Envision them, reacting gently and yourself feeling better understood and supported.

- Continue to breathe into your capacity to meet your energetic needs and make those needs known to others.

"Nothing Time"

- Set aside a minimum of one hour of time with absolutely nothing scheduled
- Sit down, breathing into the moment. Tell yourself, "this is my time. I have nowhere to be, nothing to do; I do not need to feel rushed."
- Allow your deepest intuition to guide your next step. Do whatever comes to mind first
- While you proceed with your "nothing time," allow your breath to guide every move

Discovering your Support System

- Bring your attention to the present moment, focusing on your breath
- Ask yourself, "Who of the people I know understands and embraces me for who I truly am?"

- Breathe with each name that comes up, allowing loving-kindness and appreciation for that person to flow through your body
- Ask yourself, "Who in my life encourages me to reach my full potential?
- Repeat the action of breathing with each name that arises
- Ask yourself, "Who in my life do I feel most at rest with?"
- Repeat the action of breathing with each name that arises
- Continue to breathe, saying to yourself, "These are my people. This is my support system. I will allow myself to lean on them when I need to."

Glowing Love-Energy

- Find a restful position and begin to breathe
- Imagine the aura of your energy field. How big is it? What color is it?
- Say to yourself, "I am pure love. I have room to love the entire universe and everything in it."
- Continue to repeat this phrase with every breath. Picture the aura expanding and glowing brighter

Jaguar Spirit Animal Protection

- Bring yourself into the present moment with deep breathing
- From the depth of your being, say, "I call on the spirit of the jaguar to protect me."

- Feel the reverberations of the jaguar's protection through your body, aiding you in repelling negative energy and toxicity
- Imagine a fierce, beautiful guard of your energy field, encircling you with fierce love and security

Energetic Breathing (1-3-minute meditation)

- Take some space away from your everyday life (in the bathroom, in the car, etc.) to just breathe
- Implement the 5-5-7 breathing technique
- With every breath in, say to yourself, "I breathe in pure energy."
- With every breath out, say to yourself, "I breathe out *exhaustion, *toxicity, *negativity, etc."
- Continue until you feel the tingle of pure energy coursing through your veins

Energetic Dancing/Movement

- Find a space where you can be alone and feel completely secure
- Play a song that stirs your soul and emotions, causing you to have a visceral reaction in the body each time you hear it
- As the song begins, close your eyes and deep breathe, maybe swaying back and forth slightly

- When you feel ready, release your body to move as it feels led. No choreography, no expectations, simply letting the movement of the moment lead your body into a state of pure surrender and release
- Surrender entirely to the moment, trusting your body to release any tension or trauma
- Give your body the space and freedom to heal, coming into energetic harmony

The Art of Saying "No"
- Close your eyes and begin to breathe deeply
- Begin to consider the things that drain your energy. Perhaps you have a tendency to overcommit or find yourself stuck in a relationship or circumstance that no longer serves you. Breathe with each of these places where you feel stuck
- Say to yourself "I have the power to say 'no.'"
- Imagine yourself having the necessary conversation, turning down the opportunity, or simply choosing to remove yourself from the situation
- Feel the power of saying no and being in full control of where you place your energy

The Restorative Power of Letting Go

- Breathe deeply, cultivating a sense of full peace and security
- Ask yourself, "Where are the parts of me that I need to get back?"
- Take notice of every person or place that comes to mind as still having a part of your energy and your essence
- If there are any feelings of melancholy, nostalgia, resentment, shame, or anger, allow them to be there, breathing as they flow through you
- Say to yourself, "I release this *person or place*. I reclaim what they have that is rightfully mine."
- Continue to breathe into this empowerment

Conclusion

The Path to Wellness serves as a guidebook to integrating some of the most overlooked, yet most crucial, elements of human well-being into your daily life. By providing explanations of mindfulness, chakras, and energy healing, along with an 8-week journal prompt curriculum and 50 mini-meditations, this book provides you with all the tools you need to unlock your fullest potential and deepest joy in life. The book sheds light on the factors of well-being which are largely ignored by society, and the implications these factors have on people's mental, physical, and spiritual well-being. Complete with the ins and outs of each topic in a comprehensive format, the book serves as an easy-to-follow introduction to the topics of mindfulness, chakras, and energy healing in the pursuit of holistic health. The daily guided meditations and journal prompts provided will help to bring you in touch with yourself and help you develop a larger understanding of the topics at hand. The 5- mini-meditations provided throughout the book may be integrated as needed throughout the day to regulate your energies and bring yourself into the present moment. It is our hope that this book provided you with information beyond the general scope of mental and physical wellness by drawing a map to your inner self and the deeper roots of struggle within human life. Additionally, we hope after reading this book, you feel armed with both the insight and the tools to activate mindfulness, chakra knowledge, and energy healing in order to start living your best and most balanced life.

PART III

Chapter 1: Beginner Poses

Hands to Heart

Sukhasana

Level: Beginner

Position: Sitting

Style: Restorative, Stretch

Chakra: Root

Element: Earth Element

Anatomy Focus: Chest

In a seated position, cross your shins, widen your knees and slowly pull each foot onto the opposite thigh. Allow your knees to slowly relax towards the floor. Try not to force the movement. Let gravity do the work. Straighten your back and take a deep breath. Slowly exhale through your mouth. Place your hands together, palms touching, in front of your chest. Relax your shoulders and take another deep breath in and out through your mouth. Sukhasana can be practiced at the beginning as well as at the end of your yoga routine.

Tree

Vrksasana

Level: Beginner

Position: Standing

Style: Balance, Stretch, Strength

Chakra: Third Eye

Element: Light, Water, Earth

Anatomy Focus: Hamstrings, Hips, Knees, Quadriceps

Begin in a standing position, feet hip-width apart. Inhale and slowly bend one leg and place the bottom of the foot on the opposite inner thigh. Place your hands in Namaste, palms together in front of your chest. Exhale as you raise your hands above your head. Inhale and exhale. Gently bring your hands down to your side and lower your foot flat on the ground.

Staff

Dandasana

Level: Beginner

Position: Sitting

Style: Restorative, Stretch

Chakra: Solar Plexus, Sacral, Root

Element: Fire, Water, Earth

Anatomy Focus: Lower Back, Hips, Pelvis

In a seated position, inhale and exhale, straighten both legs in front of your body. Point both toes toward the sky and lower the back of both knees toward the floor. Straighten your spine, lower your shoulders and let the palms of your hands relax beside your hips. Practice breathing at a normal pace, loosening the leg muscles as you inhale and exhale.

Side Angle

Utthita Parsvakonasana

Level: Beginner

Position: Standing

Style: Side-Bend, Balance

Chakra: Heart, Sacral, Root

Element: Air, Water, Earth

Anatomy Focus: Arms and shoulders, Lower Back, Upper Back, Hamstrings, Chest, Hips, Knees, Pelvic, Psoas, Quadriceps

Begin this position in Star Pose. While rooted in Star Pose, point your right foot away from your body. Point your left foot forward, tighten your hips, engage your core and begin to bend your right knee. Inhale and exhale. Slowly shift your body to the right. As you bend, make sure that your knee is directly over your right foot. Adjust your left foot as needed to maintain balance and proper alignment. Bend your body to the right over your right knee and place your right hand firmly on the floor in front of your foot. Lift your left hand above your head and bring your gaze past your fingertips. Continue breathing normally and move back into Star pose. Keep both feet rooted firmly in the ground.

Downward Dog

Adho Mukha Svanasana

Level: Beginner

Position: Standing

Style: Inversion, Forward-Bend, Stretch, Strength

Chakra: Third Eye, Throat, Heart, Solar Plexus

Element: Light, Ether, Air, Fire

Anatomy Focus: Arms and Shoulders, Lower, Middle and Upper Back, Biceps and Triceps, Core, Feet and Ankles, Hamstrings

Begin in a standing position and lower your hands to the ground, palms placed firmly on the mat. Walk your hands out to 45 degree angle. Inhale and exhale, engaging your core and lowering your neck and head toward the mat. Turn your gaze in between your legs as you place your chin to your chest. Tighten the stomach muscles as you continue to inhale and exhale at a steady pace. Continue pointing your lower body toward the sky as you relax into the position. Inhale and exhale walking your hands back toward your body and slowly roll up to a standing position.

Upward Facing Dog

Urdhva Mukha Svanasana

Level: Beginner

Position: Prone

Style: Back-bend, Stretch, Strength

Chakra: Throat, Heart, Solar Plexus, Sacral, Root

Element: Ether, Air, Fire, Water, Earth

Anatomy Focus: Arms and Shoulders, Lower and Middle Back, Biceps and Triceps, Core, Chest, Neck, Pelvic, Psoas

Start your pose in a prone position on your mat. Relax the stomach muscles. Inhale and exhale. Place both palms flat in front of you with your elbows bent. Press both thighs onto your mat and slowly press your hands down and lift your chest. Continue to inhale and exhale lifting until your arms and straighten your elbow. Keep both arms close to your body. Let your feet relax as you ease into the pose, breathing at a continuous pace. Slowly bend your elbows and lower your chest back down to your mat.

Thunderbolt

Vajrasana

Level: Beginner

Position: Sitting

Style: Stretch

Chakra: Third Eye, Sacral, Root

Element: Light, Water, Earth

Anatomy Focus: Feet and Ankles, Knees

In a seated position, straighten both legs out in front of your body. Inhale and exhale, straightening your spine, lowering both shoulders and tightening your core muscles. Gently bend your left leg behind your body so that your foot meets your gluteus. Repeat the same movement with your right leg. Let your buttocks relax down onto both feet and place your palms on both quadriceps. Close your eyes and continue to breath at a steady pace relaxing your upper body with each inhale and exhale.

Child's

Balasana

Level: Beginner

Position: Prone

Style: Restorative, Forward-Bend, Inversion

Chakra: Crown, Third Eye, Solar Plexus, Sacral, Root

Element: Thought, Light, Fire, Water, Earth

Anatomy Focus: Lower Back, Feet and Ankles, Hips, Knees, Neck

Begin by sitting in the Thunderbolt Pose. Raise your buttocks, widen your feet and lower your buttocks back down to the floor. Keep your calves and feet close to the body. Inhale and exhale folding forward and placing your forehead gently on your mat. Continue to inhale and exhale moving your arms behind you resting them next to your thighs. Palms facing up, allow both shoulders to slowly drift toward the mat. Continue breathing at a normal pace in this position and then slowly return to a seated Thunderbolt pose.

Warrior I

Virabhadrasana I

Level: Beginner

Position: Standing

Style: Stretch, Twist, Strength

Chakra: Throat, Heart, Solar Plexus, Sacral, Root

Element: Ether, Air, Fire, Water, Earth

Anatomy Focus: Lower and Middle Back, Hamstrings, Chest, Hips, Knees, Neck, Psoas, Quadriceps

Begin in Mountain Pose. Inhale and exhale and step your right foot behind your body. Place it firmly on your mat at a 20 degree angle to create the proper balance. Bend your left leg in front of your body. Make sure that your knee is placed directly above the top of your foot. Lift both arms directly above your head placing your biceps close to your ears. Continue breathing at a normal pace. Lower both shoulders and shift your gaze past your fingertips. Slowly, bring your right leg back to meet your left leg, straighten your spine and lower both arms.

Warrior II

Virabhadrasana II

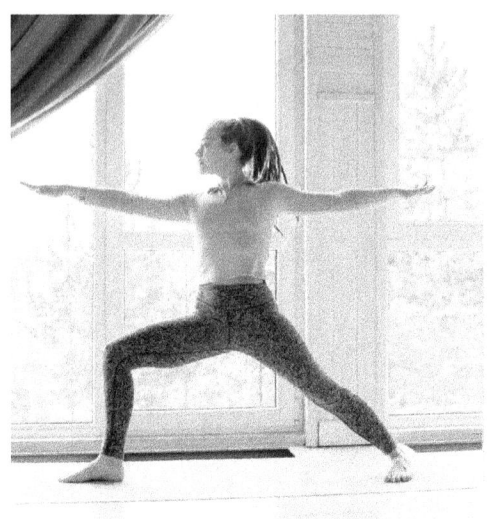

Level: Beginner

Position: Standing

Style: Stretch, Strength, Balance

Chakra: Sacral, Root

Element: Water, Earth

Anatomy Focus: Arms and Shoulders, Lower and Middle Back, Hamstrings, Chest, Hips, Knees, Psoas, Quadriceps

Begin in Mountain Pose. Inhale and exhale repositioning into Star Pose. Place both feet further than hip width apart and raise both arms to shoulder level. Point your palms down to the ground. Point your right foot away from the body and position your left foot facing forward. With your arms out wide, inhale and exhale tightening your core stomach muscles. Slowly shift your torso to the right, bending the right knee and placing it directly over the top of the foot. With a fluid movement, twist your upper body to the right and shift your gaze past your fingertips. Inhale and exhale reversing the movement to return to Star position. Gently move both feet to meet each other landing back in Mountain Pose.

Mountain

Tadasana

Level: Beginner

Position: Standing

Style: Restorative, Balance

Chakra: Sacral, Root

Element: Water, Earth

Anatomy Focus: Feet and Ankles

Standing with your feet together, straighten your spine and drop your hands to your hips. Let your shoulders relax, inhale and exhale. Engage your lower body, hips and core, pulling your navel softly toward your spine. Let your arms relax on either side of your body. Inhale through your nose and out through your mouth.

Star

Utthita Tadasana

Level: Beginner

Position: Standing

Style: Stretch

Chakra: Sacral, Root

Elements: Water, Earth

Anatomy Focus: Arms and Shoulders, Chest, Hips

Begin in Mountain Pose. Inhale and exhale widening your feet beyond hip distance. Position the soles of the feet flat on the floor. Make sure each toe is firmly placed on the ground. Lift your spine, lower both shoulders and engage your core. Tighten both legs and center the hips aligning the body for proper balance. Inhale and exhale at a normal pace and lift both arms to shoulder height. Point your fingers, palms facing downwards and lower your shoulders away from your ears. Continue breathing. Close your eyes if desired. Inhale and exhale letting your mind focus on the outward positioning while tightening your core at the same time.

Corpse

Savasana

Level: Beginner

Position: Supine

Style: Restorative

Chakra: Crown, Heart

Elements: Thought, Air

Anatomy Focus: Lower Back

Begin in a seated position with both legs straight in front of your body. Lower both shoulders, tuck your lower back and place your chin to your chest. Reach both arms in front of your upper body. Inhale, exhale and slowly roll down to a supine position. Rest both arms wide beside your body with palms facing the sky.

Let your feet fall the side. Allow the backs of your legs to loosen. Let your spine, neck and head melt into the mat as your breathing slows to a natural rhythm.

Butterfly

Baddha Konasana

Level: Beginner

Position: Sitting

Style: Stretch

Chakra: Sacral, Root

Element: Water, Earth

Anatomy Focus: Lower Back, Feet and Ankles, Hamstrings, Hips, Knees, Pelvic

In a seated position, lift your spine and straighten both legs in front of your body. Inhale and exhale. Bend both legs until the bottom of your feet are facing one another in front of your torso on your mat. Allow your legs to slowly relax into the seated position. Grip the each big toe with your hands. Inhale and exhale as you gently bend forward. Gaze down toward your toes. Continue inhaling and exhaling as you slowly straighten your spine back to your seated position.

Hero

Virasana

Level: Beginner

Position: Sitting

Style: Stretch

Chakra: Sacral, Root

Element: Water, Earth

Anatomy Focus: Hips, Knees, Quadriceps

Begin in Table Top position. Sit back on your buttocks resting in between both knees. Place both hands on your quadriceps, palms down. Inhale and gently lower your chin to your chest. Exhale and let your hips relax into the seated position. Continue to inhale and exhale making sure to keep your shoulders lowered and away from your ears.

Side Angle

Utthita Parsvakonasana

Level: Beginner

Position: Standing

Style: Side-Bend, Balance

Chakra: Heart, Sacral, Root

Element: Air, Water, Earth

Anatomy Focus: Arms and shoulders, Lower Back, Upper Back, Hamstrings, Chest, Hips, Knees, Pelvic, Psoas, Quadriceps

Begin this position in Star Pose. While rooted in Star Pose, point your right foot away from your body. Point your left foot forward, tighten your hips, engage your core and begin to bend your right knee. Inhale and exhale. Slowly shift your body as you bend stopping as your knee arrives directly over your right foot. Adjust your left foot as needed to maintain balance and proper alignment. Bend your body to the right over your right knee and place your right hand firmly on the floor beside your foot. Lift your left hand above your head and bring your gaze past your fingertips. Continue with a normal breathing pattern as you move back into Star pose, keeping both feet rooted firmly in the ground.

Garland

Malasana

Level: Beginner

Position: Standing

Style: Stretch

Chakra: Sacral, Root

Element: Water, Earth

Anatomy Focus: Lower Back, Hamstrings, Hips, Pelvic

Begin in Mountain pose, lift your spine and engage your core. Bring your hands to Namaste, inhale and gently bend both knees lowering your buttocks to the floor. Balance on your feet and rest both elbows on your inner thighs. Inhale and exhale as you slowly place both palms on the floor to push back up to standing position. Continue breathing at a normal pace.

Cobbler

Baddha Konasana

Level: Beginner

Position: Sitting

Style: Stretch

Chakra: Sacral, Root

Anatomy Focus: Lower Back, Feet and Ankles, Hamstrings, Hips, Knees, Pelvic

In a seated position, begin with your feet and legs in front of you. Inhale and exhale as you bend both knees until the bottom of your feet are touching. Allow both feet to relax on the floor and grasp each big toe firmly with your hands. Inhale and exhale stretching both knees further toward the floor. Place both of your elbows on your thighs, bend forward gazing toward your feet. Inhale and exhale and lift your spine back to a seated position.

Chair

Utkatasana

Level: Beginner

Position: Standing

Style: Forward-Bend, Stretch, Strength, Balance

Chakra: Throat, Sacral, Root

Element: Ether, Water, Earth

Anatomy Focus: Arms and Shoulders, Lower Back, Hips, Knees, Pelvic, Quadriceps

Begin in Mountain pose. Move your feet together so that they are touching. Plant both feet firmly in the ground, focusing on the heels as well as each toe. Inhale and exhale engaging your core, lowering your shoulder and tightening the glute muscles. Bend both knees. Make sure the knees are positioned directly above the feet. Continue to inhale and exhale, lowering the buttocks slightly. Lift both arms above your head and let both biceps rest near your ears. Lower both shoulders and shift your gaze upward past your fingertips. Hold this position as you inhale and exhale. Allow the upper body to gently rest upon the lower body.

Cat

Marjaryasana

Level: Beginner

Position: Prone

Style: Forward-Bend

Chakra: Solar Plexus

Element: Fire

Anatomy Focus: Lower and Middle Back, Neck

In a seated position, move into Table Top Pose resting your body on your hands and knees. Inhale and exhale and tighten your stomach muscles. Position your feet behind you and place both palms firmly on the mat. Engage each fingertip for the proper balance and alignment. Inhale and curve your back upwards, pulling your stomach in toward the spine. Tuck your chin to your chest, relax your shoulders and exhale. Lower your back to its resting Table Top position. Continue this movement inhaling and exhaling rounding your back and loosening the back muscles.

Cow

Bitilasana

Level: Beginner

Position: Prone

Style: Back-Bend

Chakra:

Element:

Anatomy Focus: Lower Back, Knees, Neck

In a seated position, move into Table Top Pose resting your body on your hands and knees. Inhale and exhale while tightening your stomach muscles. Position your feet behind you and place both palms firmly on the mat. Engage each fingertip for the proper balance and alignment. Inhale and bring your stomach toward the floor and curving the back into a U-shape. Lift your chin and stretch your neck and face toward the sky. Lower both shoulders and exhale. Return to table Top position. Continue this movement with slow deep breaths to release tension in the lower back muscles.

Side Lunge

Skandasana

Level: Beginner

Position: Sitting

Style: Stretch, Balance

Chakra: Sacral, Root

Element: Water, Earth

Anatomy Focus: Feet and Ankles, Hamstrings, Hips, Knees, Pelvic, Quadriceps

The Side Lunge can begin in Mountain Pose or continued from the Low Lunge pose. Slowly lower your body to the floor, supporting yourself with both hands and fingertips in front you on your mat. As you lower down, bend your right leg and rest your inner thigh on the top of your right heel. Point your left leg straight out to the side of your body resting your heel on the floor, left toes pointing to the sky. Continue inhaling and exhaling engaging your stomach muscles, lowering your shoulders and tightening your glutes.

Sphinx

Niravalasana

Level: Beginner

Position: Prone

Style: Back-Bend

Chakra:

Element:

Anatomy Focus: Lower Back, Biceps and Triceps, Chest

Begin in prone position. Bend both elbows keeping them close to your body, palms pushing into your mat. Keep both feet together and gently push your upper body off of your mat utilizing the triceps. Make sure to relax your neck, inhaling and exhaling during the entire stretch. Feel your stomach muscles engage toward your mat with each breath. Slowly lower back down to your met.

High Lunge

Ashta Chandrasana

Level: Beginner

Position: Standing

Style: Stretch, Strength, Balance

Chakra: Sacral, Root

Element: Water, Earth

Anatomy Focus: Arms and Shoulders, Lower and Upper Back, Hamstrings, Hips, Knees, Psoas, Quadriceps

From Downward Dog or Mountain Pose, lift both arms above your head keeping them close to your ears. Relax the shoulders. Bend your left knee and step your right foot behind your body landing on your toes. Make sure your left knee is directly above the top of the foot. And, keep your right knee slightly bent with the weight on the bottom of your right foot. Inhale and exhale continuously. Tuck your torso and engage your core on the exhale. Step your right foot forward to meet your left foot, returning to Mountain pose.

Supine Twist

Supta Matsyendrasana

Level: Beginner

Position: Supine

Style: Twist, Stretch

Chakra: Sacral, Root

Element: Water, Earth

Anatomy Focus: Lower and Middle Back, Hamstrings, Hips, Knees, Neck

Begin by laying down flat on your back. Inhale and bend both knees into your chest. Flatten your lower back into the floor and relax both shoulders. Gently begin to drop both knees to one side of your body, relaxing one knee on top of the other. Lay both arms out wide and shift your gaze in the opposite direction. Inhale and exhale continuously through this stretch. Slowly bring both knees back to your chest and lower down to your mat.

Legs up the Wall

Viparita Karani

Level: Beginner

Position: Supine

Style: Restorative, Stretch

Chakra:

Element:

Anatomy Focus: Lower Back, Pelvic, Quadriceps

Find an empty wall away from mirrors or windows. Begin in supine position with both knees bent. Move your buttocks against the wall with both hands down by your side. Inhale and exhale, placing both legs flat against the wall. Relax your neck and lower back into the floor. Breath continuously through this pose allowing the blood to begin flowing in a different direction.

Sitting Forward Fold

Paschimottanasana

Level: Beginner

Position: Sitting

Style: Forward-Bend, Stretch

Chakra: Throat, Solar-Plexus, Root

Element: Ether, Fire, Water, Earth

Anatomy Focus: Lower and Upper Back, Hamstrings, Hips, Neck

While in Staff pose, inhale and tuck your chin to your chest. Engage your core and lower both shoulders. Beginning to create a curve at the top of your neck. Slowly roll forward one vertebrae at a time. Keeping both hands by your side for support, palms down. Roll down as far as your spine will allow without forcing the motion. Slowly roll back up returning to Staff pose.

Standing Forward Fold

Uttanasana

Level: Beginner

Position: Standing

Style: Forward-Bend, Stretch, Inversion

Chakra: Crown, Solar-Plexus, Sacral, Root

Element: Thought, Fire, Water, Earth

Anatomy Focus: Lower and Upper Back, Hamstrings, Hips, Neck

Begin in Mountain pose. Inhale, tuck your chin to your chest and lower both shoulders. Exhale and slowly roll down one vertebrae at a time gazing toward your toes. Allow gravity to assist with the stretch. Try not to force or push the stretch as you fold. Slowly roll back up, chin to chest, returning to Mountain pose.

Table Top

Bharmanasana

Level: Beginner

Position: Sitting

Style: Restorative

Chakra: Sacral, Root

Element: Water, Earth

Anatomy Focus: Arms and Shoulders, Lower Back, Biceps and Triceps, Knees

In Vajrasana, walk both hands out in front of your body stopping just below the shoulders. Lift up on your knees. Keep both feet on the floor. Inhale and exhale engaging your stomach muscles. Align your head and neck with your back so that your upper torso is parallel to your mat. Shift your gaze to the mat. Gently rotate back into Child's pose.

Plank

Phalakasana

Level: Beginner

Position: Prone

Style: Strength

Chakra: Solar Plexus

Element: Fire

Anatomy Focus: Arms and Shoulders, Biceps and Triceps, Core

In Downward Dog pose, plant both feet and hands firmly on your mat, utilizing all fingertips for balance. Slowly move the entire body parallel to your mat focusing weight on the toes and hands. Make sure both hands are directly below both shoulders. Inhale and exhale through each move. Gaze toward the floor shifting the hips inward. If your wrists begin to experience a painful pressure, release to your elbows keeping your hands in front of your body. Inhale and exhale. Gently fold back to Child's pose when ready.

Bridge

Setubandha Sarvangasana

Level: Beginner

Position: Supine

Style: Back-Bend, Stretch, Strength, Balance

Chakra: Crown, Third Eye, Throat, Solar Plexus

Element: Thought, Light, Ether, Fire

Anatomy Focus: Arms and Shoulders, Lower and Upper Back, Core, Chest, Hips,

Neck, Pelvic, Psoas, Quadriceps

Begin this pose in supine position. Bend both knees bringing them close to your buttocks. Place both hands by your side, palms down. Inhale and exhale, lifting the buttocks off the floor by pushing through the soles of the feet. Make sure to support your neck by keeping it flat on the mat. Lift through to your toes if desired. Slowly lower back down to your mat.

Camel

Ustrasana

Level: Beginner

Position: Sitting

Style: Back-Bend, Stretch, Balance

Chakra: Crown, Third-Eye, Throat, Heart, Solar-Plexus

Element: Thought, Light, Ether, Air, Fire

Anatomy Focus: Lower, Middle and Upper Back, Core, Chest, Knees, Neck, Pelvic, Psoas, Quadriceps

While in Thunderbolt Pose, lift to your knees, straighten your spine and lower both shoulders. Slowly place both palms behind your body, on top of each respective heel. Open the chest, inhale, and rotate back, supporting the neck. Shift your gaze toward the sky, inhale and exhale. Tightening the quadriceps, rotate back to Thurnderbolt pose.

Four Limbed Staff Pose

Chaturanga Dandasana

Level: Beginner

Position: Prone

Style: Strength

Chakra: Solar Plexus

Element: Fire

Anatomy Focus: Arms and Shoulders, Lowers Back, Biceps and Triceps, Core, Hamstrings, Pelvic

Begin this pose in Downward Dog and walk into Plank Pose. Find the correct balance on your toes and palms of your hands while gazing toward the floor. Take a few deep breaths, tighten your core muscles and slowly bend both elbows by your side, keeping them as close your body as possible. As you lower, keep your body parallel to the floor and exhale. Breathing continuously, push up through your palms, lower both knees and sit back into Child's Pose.

Cobra

Bhujangasana

Level: Beginner

Position: Prone

Style: Back-Bend

Chakra: Throat, Heart, Solar Plexus, Sacral, Root

Element: Ether, Air, Fire, Water, Earth

Anatomy Focus: Lower, Middle and Upper Back, Biceps and Triceps, Core, Psoas

Lying on your stomach in prone position with face down, inhale and exhale tightening the stomach muscles. Firmly plant the top of your feet to the ground and place your palms close to your upper abdomen. Inhale and push through your palms, raising your chest about six inches off the ground. Exhale. Slowly lower down to your mat.

Chapter 2: Intermediate Poses

Seated Twist

Marichyasana

Level: Intermediate

Position: Sitting

Style: Twist, Forward-Bend, Stretch

Chakra: Solar, Sacral, Root

Element: Fire, Water, Earth

Anatomy Focus: Arms and Shoulders, Lower and Upper Back, Biceps and Triceps, Core, Hamstrings, Hips, Neck, Quadriceps

Begin in Staff Pose with feet straight out in front of your body. Inhale and exhale as your lift your right leg toward your chest. Keep your left leg straight, inhale and twist your torso as you place your left hand on the floor behind you. Bring your right arm around your right knee and slowly bend forward. Gently lift both hands behind you and lock them together. Inhale and exhale as you lower into the final position. Slowly release your hands and return to your upright seated position.

Boat

Navasana

Level: Intermediate

Position: Sitting

Style: Forward Bend, Strength, Balance

Chakra: Solar Plexus

Element: Fire

Anatomy Focus: Lower Back, Core, Pelvic, Quadriceps

Begin in a seated position, inhale and exhale, pointing both legs out in front of your body. Slowly round your spine and engage your core muscles. Turn your gaze toward your knees. Inhale and exhale as you bring your legs 1-2 feet off the ground in a straight motion. Point your toes. Raise both arms and place your hands, palms facing in, to the outside of your knees. Inhale and exhale as your bring your arms and legs down slowly to the ground.

Wheel

Chakrasana

Level: Intermediate

Position: Supine

Style: Back-Bend, Stretch, Inversion, Strength, Balance

Chakra: Crown, Third Eye, Throat, Heart, Solar Plexus

Element: Thought, Light, Ether, Air, Fire

Anatomy Focus: Lower Back, Core, Chest, Neck, Psoas, Quadriceps

Begin in Corpse pose, a supine position. Bring the focus to your lower back and bend both knees placing the feet flat on the floor. Inhale and exhale and place both hands behind your head, palms on the floor. Point fingers toward the shoulders and rotate both wrists away from your body. Inhale. As you exhale, slowly lift your torso off the floor. Make sure to balance the weight of your body on both the palms of your hands as well as on the soles of both feet. Continue a normal breathing pattern as you find your comfort level. Set your gaze past your elbows in this position. Slowly lower your torso down the ground. Inhale and exhale returning to the supine position.

Warrior III

Virabhadrasana III

Level: Intermediate

Position: Standing

Style: Balance, Forward-Bend, Stretch, Strength, Balance

Chakra: Solar Plexus, Sacral, Root

Element: Fire, Water, Earth

Anatomy Focus: Middle Back, Core, Hamstrings, Chest, Hips, Psoas, Quadriceps

Begin in Mountain Pose. Inhale and exhale repositioning into Star Pose, feet further than hip width apart and arms raised to shoulder level. Point your palms down to the ground. Point your right foot away from the body and position your left foot facing forward. With your arms out wide, inhale and exhale tightening your core stomach muscles. Slowly shift your torso to the right, bending the right knee and placing it directly over the top of the foot. With a fluid movement, twist your upper body to the right and shift your gaze past your fingertips. Bring your left arm parallel to your right arm, palms facing one another. Twist your entire body to the right, folding your head in between your biceps and lift your left leg off the ground. Point your left foot. Inhale and exhale tightening the stomach muscles. Shift your weight as need on your left leg to find the correct balance and alignment. Point the crown of your head toward the tips of your fingers. Hold this position for a few deep breaths. Lower yyour left leg, return both arms to your side and rest back into Mountain pose.

Triangle

Trikonasana

Level: Intermediate

Position: Standing

Style: Side-Bend, Stretch

Chakra: Heart, Sacral, Root

Element: Air, Water, Earth

Anatomy Focus: Arms and Shoulders, Biceps and Triceps, Core, Hamstrings, Chest, Psoas, Quadriceps

Begin in Star Pose, feet apart. Place both arms out wide, shoulder-width apart. Turn your right foot out 90 degrees and rotate your left foot forward. Inhale and exhale tightening your core and engaging your lower back muscles. Slightly rotate your lower back forward. With arms still placed out wide, slowly rotate down the right side of your body, fingers pointing toward your shin. Slowly lower your right hand to the floor behind your leg. Reach your left arm to the sky. Shift your gaze upward past your fingertips. Continue breathing through the pose. Slowly rotate back to Star Pose. Relax your arms to your sides and walk your feet together.

Plow

Halasana

Level: Intermediate

Position: Supine

Style: Inversion, Stretch

Chakra: Crown, Third Eye, Throat, Solar Plexus

Element: Thought, Light, Ether, Fire

Anatomy Focus: Lower, Middle and Upper Back, Core, Hamstrings, Hips, Neck, Pelvic

Begin in supine position with both legs on the floor. Inhale and raise both legs to a 90 degree angle. Exhale pushing your arms and palms to the floor, rotate your legs completely over your head. Inhale and exhale as your toes touch the floor behind your head. Continue breathing through the pose. Lower both legs back to supine position.

Low Lunge

Parsva Anjaneyasana

Level: Intermediate

Position: Sitting

Style: Side-Bend, Stretch, Strength, Balance

Chakra: Sacral, Root

Element: Water, Earth

Anatomy Focus: Arms and Shoulders, Upper Back, Biceps and Triceps, Core, Chest, Hips, Knees, Psoas, Quadriceps

Follow the steps from Warrior Pose II to move into a Low Lunge. Once in Warrior Pose II, raise both arms above your head and lower your right knee to the mat. Inhale and exhale resting the entire right leg straight behind your body. Let your knee rest gently on the mat. Your left knee should be directly above the top of your foot. Continue moving through the pose by lowering your shoulders and allowing your hips to drift slowly toward your mat stretching the hamstrings. If your knee begins to feel a painful pressure, place a blanket or mat underneath to add a cushion during this pose. Inhale and exhale. Move your right leg in front of your body, lower both arms and relax back into Child's Pose as needed.

Side Plank

Vasisthasana

Level: Intermediate

Position: Sitting

Style: Balance, Stretch, Strength

Chakra: Solar Plexus

Element: Fire

Anatomy Focus: Arms and Shoulders, Biceps and Triceps, Core

Begin in Plank pose. Inhale and rotate your entire body to the right side. Lift your left arm to the sky and shift your gaze upward. Let your left foot rest firmly on your right foot. Push through your right palm for balance and alignment. Engage your stomach muscles to provide core support. Rotate back to Plank pose and sit back into Child's pose as needed.

Half Moon

Ardha Chandrasana

Level: Intermediate

Position: Standing

Style: Side-Bend, Inversion, Strength, Balance

Chakra: Sacral, Root

Element: Water, Earth

Anatomy Focus: Biceps and Triceps, Core, Hamstrings, Hips, Psoas, Quadriceps

Stand in Mountain Pose. Use a yoga block as needed. Place the block beside your mat within arm's reach. Spread both legs, turn your right foot to the right toward the block and point your left foot forward. Inhale and exhale and slowly lean to your right placing your right hand on the block, or on the floor. Raise your left leg so that it is parallel to your mat. Lift your left hand to the sky and shift your gaze past your fingertips. Return to Mountain Pose.

Dancer Pose

Natarajasana

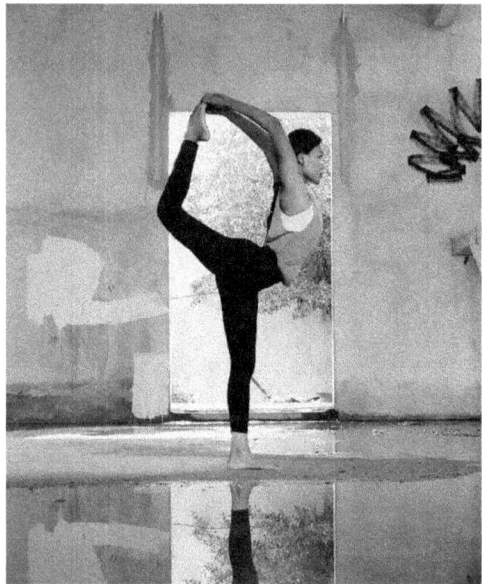

Level: Intermediate

Position: Standing

Style: Stretch, Back-Bend, Strength, Balance

Chakra: Heart, Solar-Plexus

Element: Air, Fir

Anatomy Focus: Lower Back, Biceps and Triceps, Hamstrings, Chest, Hips, Psoas, Quadriceps

Dancer Pose begins in Mountain Pose. Straighten your spine and bring your lower back slightly inward. Engage your core. Inhale and exhale bending the right knee letting the heel of your foot reach the buttocks. Stretch your right hand behind your body. Grab the toes of your right foot. Continue to inhale and exhale lifting your chest and tightening your stomach muscles. Reach your left hand straight out in front of your body. Take a deep breath in and out and twist your shoulders. Roll your fingers and thumb of your right hand around your big toe. Rotate the right elbow and shoulders allowing your arm to migrate above your head. Continue to stretch the left arm in front of you while maintaining your core balance. Plant your left foot firmly on your mat engaging the heel as well as each toe for proper balance and alignment. Slowly rotate your right arm over your head, releasing the right foot. Return to Mountain Pose.

Chapter 3: Advanced Poses

Reclined Middle Split

Supta Trivikramasana

Level: Advanced

Position: Supine

Style: Stretch

Chakra: Sacral, Root

Element: Water, Earth

Anatomy Focus: Quadriceps

Begin seated in Staff Pose. Slowly roll onto your back. Inhale and exhale planting your left leg firmly on the mat. Raise your right leg to a 90 degree angle. Grasp the big right toe and rotate your right hip. Engage the stomach muscles on the exhale and bring the right knee closer to your chest. Slowly stretch the right leg closer to your shoulder loosening the hamstrings. Release the right leg down to a supine position.

Seated Middle Split

Samakonasana

Level: Advanced

Position: Sitting

Style: Stretch

Chakra: Root

Element: Earth

Anatomy Focus: Hips, Quadriceps

Begin in a seated position, Butterfly Pose. Straighten your spine. Lower both shoulders and engage your core. Inhale and exhale widening both legs to the corner of your mat. Tuck your lower back and place both hands firmly in front of you on the mat. Lower your chin to your chest and slowly roll forward supporting your upper body with both hands. Relax into the pose letting gravity assist with the fold. Inhale and exhale. Slowly roll up one vertebrae at a time back to a seated position.

Pigeon

Kapotasana

Level: Advanced

Position: Prone

Style: Stretch, Back-Bend

Chakra: Crown, Third Eye, Throat, Heart

Element: Thought, Light, Ether, Air

Anatomy Focus: Lower and Middle Back, Core, Hamstrings, Chest, Hips, Neck, Pelvic, Psoas, Quadriceps

Begin this pose in Table Top position. Bring your left knee to meet your left wrist. Inhale and lower your left hip to the floor, supporting your body with both hands on the mat. Keep your right leg straight behind your body, knee facing the floor. Lift your chest at this point for a deep stretch. Or, slowly lower your upper body over your left knee. Relax both elbows to the mat in front of you, palms down. Inhale and exhale. Push up through the palms of your hands and lift your chest of of your knees. Return to Child's pose.

Crane

Bakasana

Level: Advanced

Position: Sitting

Style: Strength, Inversion, Balance

Chakra: Solar Plexus

Element: Fire

Anatomy Focus: Middle and Upper Back, Biceps and Triceps

Start this pose in a seated Garland pose. Inhale and exhale multiple times preparing for this pose. Place both palms on the floor engaging the triceps. Bring both knees to the chest and place them firmly in the armpit area. You will be on your tip toes at this point. Continue to allow a slight bend in both elbows. Take a few deep breaths. As you exhale, bend the torso forward lifted the buttocks in the air. Shift your weight onto your knees. Slowly lean forward pointing your forehead toward your mat. Allow both feet to lift off the mat while balancing your knees on top of your triceps. Inhale and exhale. Slowly roll back on to your feet and return to Garland Pose.

Headstand

Sirsasana

Level: Advanced

Position: Supine

Style: Inversion, Strength, Balance

Chakra: Crown, Third Eye, Throat

Element: Thought, Light, Ether

Anatomy Focus: Lower Back, Biceps and Triceps, Neck

Begin by kneeling on your mat. Rest your forearms on the mat shoulder width apart. Interlock your fingers and place the crown of your head on the mat. Cup the back of your head with your hands. After securing your head position, tuck both knees into your stomach. Inhale and exhale engaging your core and tightening the hip area. Begin to rest your weight onto your forearms and slowly lift one knee off the floor. Keep your heel close to your buttocks. Lift the opposite knee from the floor keeping both knees close to the lower body. Inhale and exhale and tightening the stomach muscles. Shift your weight off of your head and onto your elbows for balance. Slowly straighten both legs while engaging the core with every breath. Point your toes. Inhale and exhale. Gently lower one foot at a time back to a kneeling position. Slowly roll up to a final standing position.

Scorpion

Vrschikasana

Level: Advanced

Position: Prone

Style: Strength, Back-Bend, Inversion, Balance

Chakra: Crown, Third Eye, Throat

Element: Thought, Light, Ether

Anatomy Focus: Arms and Shoulders, Lower and Middle Back, Biceps and Triceps

Begin in Downward Dog. Lower both elbows down to the floor, resting both forearms on the mat. Follow the same steps as the Headstand pose to lift your feet into the air. Tuck both knees into your stomach. Inhale and exhale engaging your core and tightening the hip area. Begin to rest your weight onto your forearms and slowly lift one knee off the floor. Keep your heel close to your buttocks. Lift the opposite knee from the floor keeping both knees close to the lower body. Shift your weight onto your hands, forearms and elbows. Inhale and exhale. Slowly straighten both legs while engaging the core with every breath. Point your toes toward the sky. Inhale and exhale tightening the stomach muscles. Slowly begin to bend both knees. Point the toes toward the back of your head. Bend from the middle to upper back. Gently begin to lower one leg at a time back down to the mat. Relax back into Child's Pose.

PART IV

Chapter 1: The Clutter in Your Life

You have probably seen many shows on television about how people hoard several different items, either because they love to shop, or they have collected many articles over time and cannot bear to part with them. It gets to the point where their closets and even their entire homes are filled up completely, and it is nearly impossible to move around. You may know people like this in your own life, or perhaps, you are one of these people. If you are reading this book, then I will assume that the clutter in your space is taking over your life.

Especially in Western society, we have a fascination with material possessions of all types. If we like something, we must have it right away. As a result, we end up purchasing so many different items, and we cannot bear to part with them, even if we don't use them anymore. After several years, our living spaces and office spaces are cluttered. This includes places like the kitchen, living room, and restrooms. So many items get collected that they end up getting stored wherever they can.

You might be wondering what the big deal is. So what if I, or anyone else, collects a lot of items? Well, the stuff is yours, and you have every right to do whatever you want with it. However, what I want to address are the psychological issues that result in clutter building up in your life, as well as the effects the same clutter has on your psyche in the long run.

Why You Have Clutter

There are numerous reasons why you have so much clutter in your life. It is not as simple as forgetting to do your Spring cleaning. Even though this could be a part of it, however, there are deeper issues as well that may reflect certain aspects of your personality. This may be more common than you think because some people are able to artfully hide their clutter behind lock doors, where you will not find it unless you dig deep. You may be hiding your own clutter so that it's not visible to you. However, when you open a certain closet, a few drawers in the house, or walk into your garage or basement, and they are filled with items that you never use, then you may have an issue with clutter.

To be fair, it's almost impossible to have no clutter at all. Having a few extra items on your desk, or a drawer with some junk in the house is not a big deal. However, if it starts to cramp your personal space, then you might have a problem. I will go over some of the main reasons why people have clutter in their homes. See which ones you can relate to.

You Don't Recognize What Clutter Is

Many people allow clutter to build up in their homes because they don't recognize what it is. They have a hard time deciphering between what is valuable and what is just taking up space. Some items were once valuable but haven't been used for a long time. Because it can be hard to recognize what clutter is, people have a hard time letting anything go. They will look at something, suspect that it could come in handy down the line, and then never get rid of it.

You Don't Know How Long You Should Keep Something

This is a huge area of confusion in almost any household. How are you supposed to tell how long to keep something? Many people have no concept of when and where to let things go. I am not just talking about tools or appliances here. This can be related to anything. For example, people still have birthday or holiday cards that are decades old. It is nice to look at these cards and conjure up some nice old memories, but how many reminders of the past do you actually need?

You Don't Know How to Store Things

People often do not know how to store things. It might be because they forget, or they do not know where it should go. Suddenly, you will find something hidden in the weirdest section of your house, or worse, not be able to find it when you need it.

Along the same lines, you have no good organizing routine. Perhaps you are not an organized person, in general. This is not an indictment on you personally. Many individuals lack the ability to organize everything in their lives, and this grows worse with the more items they obtain. You can actually declutter for about

15-20 minutes a day for several days straight, and many of your items will disappear.

You Are Not Using Clutter Busters

Clutter busters are items, such as trays, baskets, jars, hooks, or folders, that can be used to place your materials in specialized locations. Yes, you will still have the items in your home, but at least they won't be in your way all the time. Can you imagine having a toilet brush on your coffee table? I certainly hope not.

Buying Too Many Things, You Don't Need

This is probably the most obvious one. How many of us don't buy things we don't need? From aspirational shopping to impulse buying, our homes are filled with things we bought on a whim. Aspirational shopping comes from our interest in actually doing something, only to realize it's not for us. However, we don't take the time to get rid of the items afterward. For example, we might watch a musician playing the guitar and want to be like him. So, we buy a guitar, end up hating it, or get to busy to practice, and then put it in a closet somewhere.

If you genuinely have an interest in learning something, I think it's great. But at least stick to it for a little while to give it a chance. If you end up not liking it, then sell the items or donate them to someone who will use them.

You Can't Let Things Go

In this last instance, you may know you are a clutter bug, and may not want to be one, but you can't seem to let things go. You have a weird attachment to them and might not know why. This will require a deeper understanding of who you are and why particular items are hard to let go, even if you never use them.

Assess your own situation and determine which of these reasons are causing you to hold onto clutter. It might be a combination of things, which is fine. The important thing is to recognize why the spaces in your life seem so busy when they do not have to be.

Endowment Effect

There is a phenomenon known as the endowment effect, which can also explain why people have a hard time getting rid of things. This is a type of bias that occurs when people overvalue something simply because they own it. It might have been given to them, or they bought it years ago, but would never consider getting it now. However, since they own it, they place a greater worth on it.

This psychological bias has resulted in many people not being able to part with something. They are not even willing to sell it at a fair price, because they feel no one will pay the real value of it. The ironic part is the person with the attachment would never consider buying the article for nearly the same price they are trying to sell it for. For example, if they have a special coffee mug, they will put it on the market for $10, but if they saw the mug in a store, they will not even consider purchasing it. It seems that ownership gives people a certain sense of power, and they hate giving it up.

There is also a concept in psychology known as loss aversion. This is where people feel the pain of losing something at a higher intensity than the joy of gaining something of equal value. For example, if a person loses five dollars, but then finds five dollars somewhere else, the original pain of losing money will still affect them more than the joy of finding money. This can be another reason the endowment effect is so powerful. If a person owns an item, getting rid of it in exchange for the actual value will not be acceptable to them. Therefore, individuals who are impacted by this mindset will overly price something to compensate for their feelings of loss.

The endowment effect is an interesting bias that is still being studied today. It is not completely understood why this mindset affects people. But it definitely does.

The Consequences of Too Much Clutter

While you may think that too much clutter just means you will have a hard time moving around stuff, the consequences actually go much deeper than that. There are numerous negative results that happen due to excess clutter, and some of them might surprise you. After this, you will probably be more motivated to clean up a little bit.

Your Stress Levels Increase

People who live in cluttered environments have higher levels of stress and fatigue. Even increased amounts of the stress hormone, cortisol, was found in their blood. Because individuals stayed in these environments, their cortisol levels never dropped throughout the day, causing chronic stress, more chronic disease risks, and even greater mortality risk.

Your Diet Is Impacted in A Negative Way

Psychological studies have also shown that people who live in more orderly environments tend to choose healthier snack options that those in cluttered areas. Since stress leads to unhealthy snacking, being around too much clutter will lead to poor dietary habits. People also tend to overeat with too much stress.

You Can Develop More Respiratory Issues

Homes that are cluttered tend to attract more dust because there are extra physical items it can settle on top of. Extra dust in the air can eventually lead to respiratory issues in the long run, and can also exacerbate active problems, like asthma or COPD.

The more items you have inside your home, the more dust is generated. This will also attract dust mites. Furthermore, if your clutter gets way too excessive, then several areas of your home will become exceedingly difficult to reach and clean. As a result, more dust will build up. Of course, respiratory issues can lead to even more health consequences.

Your Safety Is Threatened

Too much clutter can lead to an unsafe environment where people can trip and fall easily. You also have more items to bump into when you can't see. In addition, it can be difficult to move around, and essential exits might be blocked. This causes a huge risk if you ever have to evacuate your home urgently. A fire can also spread much more quickly if you have a lot of combustible items lying around.

Your Love Life Is Jeopardized

Clutter can negatively affect marriages, too, as people who have difficulty parting with things may build resentment in their spouse. The clutter does not just impact you, but everyone else in your home too. If the person you love is bothered by the clutter and you're not, then your marriage can definitely suffer.

If you are not married and just dating, imagine what your date would think if she saw your home, and it is completely disorganized. If they don't run for the hills right away, they might do so as soon as the date is over.

Your Kids Will Be Upset

Yes, your kids, who you constantly tell to clean their room, will be upset with excess clutter. Studies have found that kids who live in a cluttered environment tend to have more distress, which will affect other areas of their lives.

You Will Become Isolated

A large number of adults say they won't invite anyone over to their house if they feel it is too messy. If you have a lot of clutter and you feel this way, then you likely have not had many guests in your house recently. This can cause you to become isolated from the world, especially if you are a homebody. If you like to spend all of your time outside of your home, then I guess this one won't be too relevant for you.

A person who lives in clutter rarely confines these tendencies to their home life. They will carry them everywhere, including their work environment, as you will see with some of the following examples.

You Will Miss Out On Getting Promoted

Untidiness at work, including a messy desk, a chaotic briefcase, or an unorganized filing system, can have negative impacts on your job performance. You will likely spend too much time looking for things and not enough time actually doing any work. Your boss will notice your clutter as well, and this can put you in a bad light when it's time to hand out promotions. According to a study on the career website, CareerBuilder, roughly 28% of employers are less likely to promote someone who keeps their workspace messy. They feel that disorganization leads to poor job performance, and they are right to think this way.

You Are More Likely to Miss Work

The National Institute of Mental Health studies have found that individuals in a cluttered environment are more likely to miss work. They estimated an average of seven missed days per month, which is an excessive number.

Your Productivity Decreases

While you are in a cluttered environment, your ability to focus is severely impeded. If you have many different items within your visual field simultaneously, they all compete for your brain's attention. You cannot give it equally to all of them, so you focus more on things that you are interested in. More often than not, that usually not your work projects. If you have papers, pens, food, and various other things on your desk, you will have a hard time getting any work done at all, and your productivity will be greatly affected. Once again, the bosses will take notice, and you won't be in very high standing when they hand out raises or promotions. In fact, they may not keep you at all if you're not performing as you should.

See how many negative results can happen to your career by keeping your workspace too cluttered? It will behoove you and your career aspirations to change this quickly.

You Will Develop Poor Spending Habits

When you live in a cluttered environment, it can become difficult to find things. As a result, you will buy another item of the same kind, not realizing it was hiding under all of your rubbish.

You Can Go into Debt

This last one may not be relevant anymore due to the ability to make online payments, but those of you who rely on paper bills as a reminder to pay them will suffer greatly. Bills become lost and forgotten, resulting in extra fees. If these are really important bills like credit cards or house payments, then additional problems will occur with the banks and financial institutions. Even your credit score will start to decline.

As you can see, the various negative effects of too much clutter can impact every area of your life. It can significantly decrease your physical and mental health and create many psychological issues for you. With the impact on career and relationships too, you will fall further down into the abyss.

Think about your own life and determine how much of an effect clutter has on your mindset. I am willing to bet that you feel much better sitting in a particular area after you have cleaned it up a little bit. Now that we have established some reasons why people collect clutter and the negative consequences associated with it, I will go over some action steps to get rid of clutter in your life.

Clutter is Not Just Physical

I have spoken a lot about the physical clutter around your home or office. All of this is very distracting and can cause you to lose focus. Too many stimuli will compete for your focus, and you will not be able to give any of them your full attention. Important issues will go right over your head.

Physical clutter is bad, but it is not the only kind you have to contend with. Clutter also includes technology, which is a growing problem in this day and age. We get emails all the time from many different sources. Sometimes we don't even know who the email is from, and just ignore it. However, we often don't erase the email or unsubscribe from the individual, which results in even more unnecessary items in our inbox. Junk email is literally regular junk mail on steroids. When we get so many different ones from various sources, it clutters our files, and we become extremely overwhelmed, just like with physical clutter. As a result, a lot of important information falls through the cracks.

With so much information coming in, it becomes very distracting, and our ability to focus and remain productive decreases. Once we become overwhelmed, we no longer answer emails; we simply scroll through them and hope we did not miss anything important. Suddenly, an important email from our boss comes through, and we never catch it. As a result, critical information was missed, which can jeopardize your company and even your job.

Digital clutter is not exclusive to too many emails. Having an excessive number of programs or apps on your computer, carrying around multiple devices, managing multiple social media accounts, and storing a lot of photos can also be overwhelming in the same manner. In many cases, once a person's data gets used up, they just buy more space, rather than clearing out what they have. It's usually quicker and easier that way. It may not seem like a big deal in the present moment, but after a few months or years, you will realize just how much your productivity and focus has decreased. Increasing productivity and getting things done will be a major topic of this book.

Chapter 2: Breaking Your Relationship With "Stuff"

Now that we have established the psychological reasons people hold onto things, it is to incorporate strategies that will help you get rid of excess clutter. While decluttering can be very difficult at first, it can also be very freeing and have a positive impact on your life in every way. In this chapter, I will go over various different techniques for you to start reducing your personal items or reorganizing them in a proper fashion. Either way, your home, and workspace will become more appealing and habitable.

Getting Over the Endowment Effect

Since the Endowment effect has such a great impact on your ability to get rid of things, I will go over some tips to help you overcome it. Once you go through these steps, you will realize how little value the items in your life actually have and how ridiculous it was to hold onto them for so long when you weren't using them.

The following are a few simple ways to get over the endowment effect:

- Well, now that you know what the endowment effect is, you can become aware that it is personally affecting your life. If you are having difficulty letting go of something you don't need, tell yourself it's the endowment effect and break the curse.

- Using your imagination can help here too. If you are having a hard time getting rid of something, imagine that you do not own it anymore. This can help weaken the emotional ties you have to it.
- Take the items you no longer use and put them in a sealed box. Now, put them somewhere like an attic or basement. Give yourself a timeline, like three months or six months, and if you do not open that box, then give it away without unsealing it.
- Write down your "why." Why is it important for you to declutter, and what value will it bring to your life?

These tips will help you overcome the power that the endowment effect holds on you, and it should become a little easier to declutter your life after this.

More Decluttering Tips

In this section, I will go over some more decluttering tips to help you reorganize your life. You can use one, or all of these, to start getting rid of unnecessary items. Through some of these steps, you can also determine which items you still need and the ones you can get rid of without a thought.

- Make the process less overwhelming if you are new. Start with five minutes a day and use this time to declutter what you can. From here, raise the time at your comfort level.

- Give one item away each day. By the end of week one, you will have given away seven items. By the end of the year, you will have given away 365. You will definitely see your belongings disappearing quickly. If you want to make the process faster, you can certainly increase the amount you give away.
- Get a large trash bag and fill it up with as many items as you can. After filling it up, tie the bag and donate to Goodwill or another donation service before you change your mind.
- Take all of your clothes and hang them facing backward. Whenever you wear an item, hang them back up facing forward. After several months, the clothes that are still facing backward should be donated.
- Use the 12-12-12 rule for getting rid of items. Take out 12 things that you plan on donating, 12 things that you plan to throw away, and 12 things that you will keep for now. This will lessen the impact of getting rid of things because you can see what you're still keeping.
- Go into your home with a first-time visitor mindset. Look around the house and determine how you would clean and reorganize the place, including what items you would get rid of. This is a mind trick you can use to detach yourself from the things inside.
- Choose a small area of your home and take before and after pictures. For example, take a small section on your kitchen counter that has clutter, snap a quick photo, and then clean off the area. Take another photo right after that. Having this visual will help you keep that area clear. Start doing this with other areas of your home too.

Decide whichever tip works best for you and then go from there. If there are others that you come up with, that is fine too. The goal is to declutter in whatever way necessary, so get creative in your approach.

Stop Buying Stuff You Don't Need

If you are decluttering the stuff out of your personal space, but also buying things you don't need at the same time, then it defeats the purpose. You are just replacing one set of items for another. As a result, decluttering will mean nothing as your environment will just become busy again. The goal of decluttering is to keep your space from becoming overfilled. This requires a combination of getting rid of stuff and not buying new stuff. The following are some effective ways to stop buying unnecessary items.

Keep Away from Temptations

If you have a tendency to splurge on things you don't need, then don't tempt yourself by window shopping or going into a store to look around. You might also want to stop getting shopping magazines and cancel online subscriptions to stores. You may not be thinking about buying an item until you see it, and then suddenly, it is in your room just sitting there.

If you must go to the store, make a list and stay laser-focused on it. If you know where the items are, then only go to those sections of the store. You can also shop online and have the items delivered, so you don't actually go out.

Avoid Retail Seduction

Retail stores are masterful at seduction, from hiring the best salespeople, to proper lighting, placement, and layout. All of this is done to draw in their customers, and many people fall for it. This is why someone ends up spending 20 dollars on a coaster set when a five-dollar one would have worked.

Avoid retail seduction by being aware of it. When you see an enticing item, mentally isolate it from its environment and see if the appeal is still there. Also, imagine it being placed in a bin at the thrift store and see if you still want to buy it.

Take Inventory

Oftentimes, we buy things because we don't have enough. However, if you take regular inventory of everything in your home, including inside the drawers, you will find more than you realized. The desire to buy more will go down. Even after you declutter, you will still have many items.

Practice Gratitude

Be mindful of the things you have in your life, both tangible and intangible, and show gratitude for them. Again, you will realize your life is more fulfilling than it appeared beforehand.

These are just a few tips to keep you from going on a shopping splurge and refilling your house with items that are useless. Once you see the powerful effects that decluttering will have on you, it will be lifechanging in so many ways. This is why so many people who became minimalists are much happier now.

Calculate Cost Vs. Labor

The trick here is to figure out how much something costs, and then determine how many hours you would have to work to make up that money. This can really be eye-opening for you. Determine if the labor hours are worth the item you want to purchase.

Keep Your Big Picture in Front of You

When you are spending money day-to-day, it can be easy to lose track of things. You may not realize how much one day of spending can take you away from your ultimate goals. This is why it's important to keep the big picture at the forefront of your mind. Use whatever reminders you need to accomplish this.

A lot of the techniques I have gone over about tricking your mind or shifting the mindset away from what you are used to. Incorporating all of these strategies into your life on a regular basis will give you the best results.

The Benefits Of Decluttering

The benefits of decluttering are another thing you can keep in mind to help you stay focused on eliminating excessive items from your life. The process really is freeing once you give it a chance. The following are a summary of some of the benefits of decluttering. I will get into many more over the next few sections.

- Reduced stress and anxiety related to all of the clutter.
- Reduced number of allergens, like dust, pet hair, and pollen that can accumulate on surfaces.
- A cleaner and more sanitary environment.
- Save extra money and even make money by selling things.
- Extra space in your home for fun activities.
- Less shame in inviting guests.
- Your home will be safer to move around in. There will be fewer things to run into.
- Family or others who are living with you will appreciate it.
- You will realize how many things you can actually do without.

Decluttering Equals Increased Focus and Productivity

Imagine a housecat for a moment. They easily become distracted by shiny lights, new toys, or any hanging objects. If you put something in front of a cat's face, they will be mesmerized by it. If you place multiple items in front of them, they will not be able to figure out which one to focus on. Our minds can become the same way if we let them.

Lucky for us, our brains have a natural filtering mechanism that allows it to not be distracted by every little thing around is. So, when you are performing a task, you may not notice the slight wind outside, the cars driving by on the front seat, or every single person that walks by. Our brains do a great job of shutting out what we don't need to see, hear, or feel every moment.

The problem here is, it takes a lot of energy to filter things out, and this energy is finite. This means that the more things around us that have the potential to catch our attention, the more energy the brain uses, and the more quickly it will dissipate. Therefore, the more clutter you have, the quicker your brain will lose its ability to focus, and you will become distracted more easily.

It is simple to see, then, that decluttering will increase your focus because you have fewer things that will drain the energy required to keep it. Try something as soon as you can. While you are sitting at your table, remove a few items from it and see how many less distractions you have. Remove any objects that are unnecessary to the task at hand. Many people will keep snacks at their desks. Avoid doing this because then you will just be snacking constantly, instead of working. When you're hungry, actually get up, and make yourself something. Put in the work.

Notice how much clearer your mind feels after doing this. When our surroundings become too busy, so does our mind. While some people believe that a busy mind creates productivity, it is quite the opposite. A clear mind with focus is what allows true productivity, so if you want to get things done, clear up your environment, and clear up your brain.

Decluttering and Improved Health

Decluttering will improve many aspects of your health. Notice some of the healthiest people around you, and you will see that their living or workspaces are immaculate compared to others. I will go over a few ways that decluttering will have positive health consequences.

Improved Healthy Habits

When you declutter your home, you will develop healthy habits. The main reason for this is that certain items will be easier to get to and will more likely get used. For example, if you open your closet and quickly find the vacuum or broom, you are more likely to use them. If your vacuum is behind a wall of various items, you will not want to put in the effort to get it. This goes for cooking, as well. If your kitchen is filled up with supplies, like extra appliances, cookware, dirty dishes, and various articles that don't need to be there, you are less likely to cook meals at home. There is a greater chance that you'll just cook a microwave dish or buy fast food.

Better Self-Care

When living in a clean and sanitary environment, you will have better self-care overall. It will be easier and more appealing to exercise in an open space. Also, your sleeping habits will improve because it is easier to be restful in less busy surroundings. Finally, people who declutter slowly develop the habit of remaining clean, which improves hygienic practices.

Losing Weight

This may seem like an odd connection, but it's true. People are much more likely to be overweight if they live in a cluttered environment. A study done by the University of Florida estimates about a 77 percent higher chance of being overweight or obese. This is related to the busy lifestyles that people have, which is common with people who do not declutter. When you learn to declutter, you also learn to slow down. You also become much more organized. This gives you more time to eat properly and exercise.

Easier to Relax

Too much clutter in your home can impact your ability to relax and enjoy yourself. The immense amount of distractions will ever allow your mind to stop getting distracted. It will be hard to immerse yourself in a relaxing activity, like reading, watching a movie, or taking a bath. You will just feel cramped, and trying to calm your nerves will be an uphill batter you cannot win.

All of these benefits will work in conjunction to improve your physical and mental health.

Having More Space

It is easy to see that decluttering opens up space around you. Not only will you have a greater physical area to work in, but a larger mental space to think. You will become more creative because it will be easier for you to open up your mind. This is where some of your best ideas will come into play.

Having an open space can increase your confidence and self-efficacy. A lot of this has to deal with the decluttering process. As you remove items from your life or reorganize them, you will have to make some important decisions. Getting rid of stuff is not easy, and you will have to think quite a bit. This will improve your capability to come up with solutions, which will definitely make you more confident in yourself. This will also give you more energy because you put yourself in the mode of getting things done. This relates back to productivity.

Having more open space reduces family and relationship tension. An excessive mess can lead to major arguments. Disagreements may arise over who causes the clutters, and therefore, who should get rid of it. Parents will often become frustrated with their children because it will take forever to find something. Do not underestimate how beneficial having more open space can be for your personal relationships.

Think back to when you moved into your home or office. This was prior to moving in any furniture or personal items. Even if it's a small space, it certainly looked much bigger than it appeared before adding extra items. Now, imagine how much bigger your space will become from just removing half of your stuff out. You will truly appreciate the extra space when you have it.

6-Week Decluttering Challenge

You can certainly take as long as you need to declutter your home, office, car, or other space that you occupy regularly, but using a challenge can light a fire under and hold you accountable for making some real changes. You can also bring in the help of a friend to help hold you accountable. Let them know what you plan to accomplish each week, and then bring them in at the end of every week to assess your progress. Take before and after photos, too, so you can have your own visuals.

It is a simple process. Starting from the beginning, pick a certain part of your home that you will focus on each week. For example, week one will be dedicated to the kitchen and dining room. Then, the second week will be dedicated to the living room. The third week will be dedicated to one or two bedrooms, depending on the amount of clutter. In the fourth week, the focus will be on the garage. In the fifth week, you can start on the basement. Finally, the sixth week can be used for any leftover closets or the laundry room. This is just an example, and you can make up your own plan based on your particular spaces. You can break down each week into smaller goals, as well.

Here is a visual:

- Week 1: Kitchen and dining room
    - Declutter the countertops-Day 1
    - Declutter the fridge-Day 2
    - Declutter the cabinets-Day 3
    - Declutter the pantry-Day 4
    - Declutter the stove and oven-Day 5
    - Declutter the dining room table-Day6
    - Declutter any other tables or cabinets in the dining room-Day 7

It may be best to start in the kitchen because it is a high traffic area in the house. From here, you can cover the other areas of your home and break it down day by day. It is really that simple. You just have to maintain discipline. Feel free to incorporate any of the strategies for decluttering I went over earlier.

After doing the six-week challenge, give yourself a pat on the back for your accomplishment. You can even reward yourself. In fact, you can also give yourself small rewards at the end of each week, granted that you accomplished what you needed to. If you stick to the challenge, you will not believe how much more space you will have. Your home may even look bigger than before.

Now that we have established the benefits of decluttering and how you can get this done in your life, the rest of the book will cover how to move forward and start getting things done in your life.

^

PART V

Chapter 1: Your Restorative Practice

Restorative Yoga is a calming practice. A practice that many of us need daily.

This specific type of yoga helps to release tension, anxiety and stress that stems from busy daily activities, traumatic circumstance or life-changing events. Restorative yoga typically utilizes props including blankets, bolsters, blocks, aromatherapy, etc. Props in restorative yoga assist with body alignment, relaxation and weight balance. They can also aide in alleviating pressure in certain areas of the body while practicing asanas.

Most of us are aware of the popular yoga classes that incorporate constant movement and active poses. Restorative yoga, however, utilizes the poses that allow your body to slowly stretch in to a relaxed state. Breathing techniques and meditation are incorporated into each pose prompting the body to slow down and enter a mode of stillness. These restorative poses and techniques ease symptoms related to anxiety, depression, stress, pain and trauma-related injuries.

The main ingredient in restorative yoga is time and patience. Each pose is held for a longer period of time allowing the body to enter into a state of mind-body unification. Holding the poses for a longer period of time also provides a deeper stretch, "stretching to the bone," as some would explain.

Daily life can send us reeling through a multitude of emotions. Simply going to the grocery store can ignite a high level of stress. Unexpected, life-altering events may bring about intense changes affecting the way we react to certain situations. The way we handle stressful situations can cause the physical body to remain tense with no sign of relief. The human body is capable of leading a very active life. We must take the time to give our minds and our bodies a break. If we do not, our immune system might deteriorate, and our minds will fade.

So, when do we slow down?

More importantly, how do we slow down? Once that roller coaster called life starts chugging away, most of us don't know how to stop, or how to slow down. We need some kind of assistance or daily practice that will help us to decompress.

We must stop running ourselves into the ground.

Learning how to recognize a quiet moment, a peaceful place, the sound of silence – We all long for each of those opportunities, but refuse to stop and realize that they are most likely right in front of our faces. Stillness is very important. And, the older we get, the harder it is to return to that state of stillness.

Generally speaking, yoga is defined as the unification of the mind and body. It is the practice of harmonizing the physical body with the spiritual body and returning to a conscious state of stillness and mindfulness.

When practicing the restorative method of yoga, time is a very important aspect. In restorative yoga, you will hold the asanas for 3-5x longer than in other yoga practices. Typically, in one restorative yoga session, you may only complete 3-5 poses. As opposed to an active yoga session, you may flow continuously through 10-20 poses.

Some examples of restorative yoga poses are Child's pose, Corpse pose, Legs-Up-The-Wall pose, etc. During each pose, you can incorporate very specific breathing techniques and meditation methods. Holding the poses for a longer period of time also allows you to adjust your body for proper alignment and balance.

Let's face it, we are all uniquely built. Not one of us is the same, physically, emotionally or mentally. Therefore, we must adjust our yoga practice to fit our own personal needs.

There are many ways to create your own unique restorative yoga practice.

Chapter 2: Yoga is for Everyone

First of all, let's get one thing straight. You do not have to be perfect to practice any type of yoga. Yoga is a balancing of the mind and the body. We all have very unique body types. No one is made the same. Your yoga practice is exactly just that - a practice tailored to fit the needs of your mind and your body.

You may feel

 like you are overweight, too tall, too short, not flexible, too skinny, etc. Try to let go of whatever inhibitions may be keeping you from jumping into your first routine. Many people immediately associate the word yoga with headstands and pretzel poses. While those advanced activities are certainly a piece of the yoga puzzle, they do not define yoga.

For example, let's say you have had a really rough day at the office, or with the kiddos. Maybe you are dealing with a loss in the family or financial struggles. Maybe your day, week, month or year just hasn't gone as planned. If you know the basics of yoga and how to practice on your own, you just may be able to ease that anxiety or calm the stress that comes during those difficult times.

But, hey! Maybe you are having a great day, week, month or year. That sounds wonderful, doesn't it? Then let your yoga practice serve that cherry on top. Learning the simple art of taking breaths throughout your day and mastering the act of sitting still could totally change your life.

There's nothing wrong with feeling shy at first when it comes to deciding to start your own yoga practice. But, remember, you are important and need to be healthy and happy. Taking that first step toward the local yoga studio or even just setting up a yoga mat at home could be one of the best steps of your life!

A Restorative Practice at Home

Restorative Yoga can absolutely be practiced at home.

Gyms and studios are fabulous practice areas as well. But, there may be days where you can't make it out of the house. Or, your schedule isn't permitting a quick run to the gym. Sometimes yoga studios have to reorganize their classes and you usual time slot isn't available anymore.

That's ok!

Let's create our own home studio for those days.

Follow these simple steps to begin setting up your own home practice.

1. Find a Quiet Spot - Find a space in your home away from loud noises and people. That space may be in a quiet room, in the backyard, or any peaceful spot that you choose.

2. Set the Mood - Once you have found the perfect space, dim the lights, lower the shades and turn down any loud sounds. If you enjoy a favorite scent, turn on an oil diffuser, light a candle, or burn incense.

3. Create Space - Yoga requires space. Once your yoga mat is situated, make sure to move any objects that may get in the way of your arms and legs.

4. Be Patient - Practicing yoga at home is very different than practicing in a studio. There may be times when you have to check on the kids, answer the door, check the oven, etc. That's ok. Simply deciding to begin yoga is a huge step in the right direction.

Breathing Techniques

Each yoga pose should include a breathing pattern, or breathing technique if you will. There are many types of breathing patterns to follow. It is perfectly acceptable to create a breathing pace that works best for your practice.

Let's face it, we all lack the proper amount of oxygen. We readily give in to the ease of shallow breathing throughout our busy day, and we forget to take in those absolutely necessary deep breaths.

The practice of breathing in yoga is called Pranayama.

If yoga does nothing other than prompt us to breath for an hour, then so be it. In fact, if you are a beginner yoga student, simply just learning how to breath may be the extent of your first few classes. Enjoy it, because the hard poses come next!

Practicing how to breath seems like a simple task. Just wait though. This involuntary act of breathing that we so recklessly abandon too much in a day may give you that energy boost you've been looking for. And, guess what? You can practice breathing anywhere!

So, let's breath.

Pursed Lip Breathing

1. Sit quietly and relax your neck and shoulders. Place your arms beside your body and let your hands lay on your lap or mat.

2. Inhale through your nose and hold for two counts.

3. Purse your lips as if you were drinking through a straw.

4. Gently blow your entire breath out through your lips until your abdomen releases completely.

Diaphragm Breathing

1. Lie on your back in a quiet space. You can bend your knees for comfort or simply rest both legs on the floor.

2. Place one hand on your chest and the other hand on your stomach.

3. Inhale through your nose allowing your belly to extend.

4. Exhale through your pursed lips, feeling your belly empty all of its air, releasing down into your spine.

Lion's Breathing

1. Sit comfortably in a quiet space with legs crossed and hands placed on both knees.

2. Inhale through your nose letting your chest expand. Lower both shoulders.

3. Open your mouth wide and exhale making the "Ha" sound until you've expended all of the air in your belly.

Alternate Nostril Breathing

1. Begin in a seated position

2. Lift your hand to your nose. Press your pointer and middle finger down against your palm and release the index and pinky fingers toward the sky.

3. Press your thumb against your right nostril. Closing the airway.

4. Inhale through your left nostril.

5. Release the thumb and exhale through your right nostril.

6. Repeat on the other side.

Coherent Breathing

1. Find a comfortable seated position

2. Inhale for 5 counts.

3. Exhale for 5 counts.

Any one of these breathing techniques can be performed during your restorative yoga practice. The beauty behind the art of breathing is that it can be done anywhere, preferably in a quiet and calm space.

There are, however, many times during the day where you are not able to find a quiet space. Let's say you begin to feel anxious during an important business meeting. You could quietly begin the "Coherent Breathing" technique without causing a scene.

Not only can you practice these breathing steps during a restorative yoga session, but you can also apply them in everyday situations.

Meditation Methods

Meditatiion in an intergral piece to every type of yoga practice. In fact, meditation should be an important part of each person's daily routine. There is no one way to meditate. Personal meditation practices are based each person's unique character, specific surroundings and life experiences.

There are hundreds of meditation techniques spanning many different cultures, religions and spiritual practices. Choosing a meditation method that is right for you may take time. It is important to find the right space – space where you feel comfortable enough to be yourself.

Meditation is your personal piece of art. Your thoughts during meditation are your own and belong to no one else. It is a time for you to be honest with yourself. This is your space to approach the places in your mind that are typically suppressed in real life.

There are two types of meditation – guided and unguided.

Guided meditation is exactly as it sounds. A teacher helps to guide you through the steps of a particular meditation practice. The teacher explains how the mind operates, walks you through step-by-step and assists in implementing the meditation into your daily life.

Unguided meditation simply involves one person – You. This method of meditation allows you to decide exactly where, when and how you want to practice. You are the teacher when it comes to an unguided meditation practice.

Simply put, meditation teaches focus. Our day-to-day lives are constantly filled with messages, ads, phone calls, texts, requests, deadlines, etc. Our brain never gets a moment to itself. Meditation is the art of finally stopping all the ruckus in your head and giving your personal thoughts some much needed attention.

As we continue to deal with all of these distractions, our mind becomes adept to wandering. We never get the chance to complete our thoughts. We are constantly distracted.

Meditation teaches us how to recognize when our mind begins to wander away from the initial thought. As you practice mindfulness in meditation, you learn how to bring your thoughts back to consciousness and awareness.

In restorative yoga, meditation can be used to create stillness while practicing the asanas. It helps to counteract distractions, anxious feelings, social awkwardness and negative energy.

Meditation during each restoratice yoga pose engages the mind-body unification practice that defines yoga as a whole.

Alignment and Balance – Props

Props are very important in restorative yoga. Yoga props assist physically in reaching your yoga goals. By utilizing props in your yoga practice, you are less likely to say, "I can't!"

We've all said or heard the "I can't do it" comments when it comes to yoga.

"I'm just not that flexible."

"I can't do yoga because I'm overweight."

"I'm too old."

"I had surgery years ago and just can't move the way I used to."

The best response to anyone justifying there inability to practice yoga is, "YES! You can."

Yoga isn't about practicing like everyone else. Yoga isn't about looking like the girl or guy online or in the health and fitness books.

Yoga is simply practicing like YOU practice.

There is no one human body made exactly like the other. Your hand may not reach the floor during the Side Angle pose. That's ok! You may need a yoga block under your neck during Savasana to ease your lower back pain. Maybe rolling a blanket and placing it under you knees for spine support is necessary. There is no right or wrong way to practice yoga. It's all ok!

Everyone is different.

You are unique and so shall your yoga practice be!

Restorative yoga incorporates many different props that hav different responsibilities. They are there to aide your body's alignment and balance as your move through each pose.

One important thing to remember when adding a prop to your pose, be patient. We may feel like we need to rush to grab a prop before trying a new pose. It's not important how quickly you get into the pose. Take your time. Listen first as the teacher explains the elements of the pose. Then decide whether or not you will need a prop based on how your body reacts to each movement.

If you need to come out of the pose to grab a prop, then do so. If your neck is straining, don't throw your shoulder out trying to reach the block or the blanket. Be patient with your body. Utilizing a prop should create physical and mental relaxation, not added stress.

So, what in the world are these "props" we keep mentioning. Ok, let's see what all of these crazy blocks, straps and bolsters are all about!

Blocks

Yoga blocks are made of wood, foam or cork. These blocks can support your body in many of the yoga poses. For example, you can place the block next to you during a Side Angle or Triangle pose. This allows your to place your hand on the block instead of the floor. A block can also be used as a head rest during Savasana or under your lower back during Bridge pose.

Bolster

The bolster prop is most widely used in restorative yoga. This is a reactangular cushion providing support for many heart-opening and lower back exercises. The bolster can be used under the forehead during Child's pose or under the knees in Tree Top pose.

Straps

Straps are like large rubber bands used in many "stretch" poses. They act as extensions of the arm or leg for poses such as the Dancer pose or the Wheel pose. Straps can be used during a forward fold by wrapping it around your wrists and feet assisting in the stretch.

Sandbags

Sandbags are like large bean bags used to add weight on the body for a deeper stretch. They can be used on the hips during poses such as the Supine Twist

Blanket

Blankets in yoga have many different uses. You can use a blanket as your practice mat, folded as a cushion for an elbow or a knee, or as a pillow for your head during restorative poses.

Eye Pillow

The yoga eye pillow is used to block out light and helps to calm the brain. It facilitates a deeper meditation and filter out visual distractions. It is perfect for Savasana and can sometime be scented for aromatherapy.

Mat

The yoga mat is where it all happens. Your mat can be most anything that feels comfortable to you. Some use the typical foam mat that rolls up and is easy to carry. Some yoga students like to use blankets, or a "serape." Just make sure that whatever you choose offers support, stability and comfort.

Essential Oils

Aromatherapy changes the game! There's certainly nothing wrong with a little sweat during your yoga practice. But, when it's time to relax and soothe, choosing the right essential oil scent is important. Scents such as lavender, jasmine, sage, lemongrass and vanilla are all very popular in the restorative yoga practice.

Music

Set the tone with relaxing tunes. In a world of digital downloads, it's simple and easy to add music as you flow through each restorative yoga pose.

Chapter 3: Yoga Flow

Flow yoga is a term that relates to a style of yoga focusing on patterned breathing and rhythmic movement.

Flowing through yoga is a beautiful movement. There are thousands of poses and many different sequences. That's why choosing your favorite type of yoga is a good decision. You can focus on practicing and developing the seqences or "flow" that works best for you and your body.

Yoga flow teach the body and the mind to work harmoniously together. Not only are you placing your body into specific poses, but your mind is learning to transition through to the next pose. This requires a reorganization of the mind, giving the brain a mental boost. Practicing continuous physical movement changes our thought patterns.. It helps us to get out of a rut sometimes. It also helps to boost our energy by bring on new challenges. When we train our brain to reorganize, we create a wealth of new thoughts and ideas.

Increasing mental focus and training our bodies to become stronger and more agile is very important at any age in life. Yoga flow is a low impact method used to gain strength of the mind and the body. The series of poses in a "flow" exercise, utilizes rhythmic breathing. It's very important to calculate each movement and whether or not you should be inhaling or exhaling at the same time. Your breath pattern is used to measure how long you will hold the pose. It also helps us to count through each movements during the same pose.

The process of patterned breathing while moving through a yoga sequence has many physical benefits. Breathing patterns can stabilize your heart rate, regulate body temperature and help you to maintain consistent movement all the way to the end of the exercise. Synchronizing your breath stables your heart rate and assists your body in releasing a balanced amount of heat. Therefore, your muscles will stretch and loosen properly during each exercise.

Learning yoga flow can be easy. The most important first step is to sign up for a class taught by a certified or qualified yoga instructor. It may be a good idea to initially choose a smaller class, especially if you are a true beginner in the yoga world. This way the instructor will have the time to address each student on a more personal level. He or she will have the chance to monitor your movemements. They can also personally assist you in modifying the pose based on your ability.

Attending a smaller class will also give you the opportunity to assess the space. Where should you place your mat? How much space will you need? Where are the props? Yoga flow classes also require intense focus. A smaller class can lessen the stress of unwanted distractions such as cramped space, the lack of props, phone noises, foot traffic, etc.

Obviously, the poses that you can expect in your Yoga Flow class depend on the level of the class.

Yoga levels are pretty basic – Beginner, Intermediate and Advanced. The instructor will most likely progress through a series of the same poses over a certain period of clases. Make sure to inquire about which level that you will be signing up for. There may be certain poses, positions, bends, stretches, etc. that could cause injury if you are not ready. This is true especially for back bends and inversion poses.

Yoga is a process. Everything you learn in your beginner class sets the foundation for your practice in the intermediate and advanced classes. So, sign up for that beginner class and plan to perfect the easy poses.

Your body will thank you.

Chapter 4: The Many Types of Yoga

Hatha

Hatha is the yoga practice that specifically deals with physical poses. Hatha is very common in Western culture. When people think of yoga, the physical poses immediately come to mind.

Hatha poses are slower and the movements are very calming. Yoga flow is integrated into a Hatha practice.

Also though the poses are slower and more relaxed, your body and mind still benefit from the poses. By flowing through the poses at a more relaxed pace, you can also focus on your breathing techniques and alignment during each movement. Hatha is a great practice for beginners.

Iyengar

Iyengar was the man's name who founded Iyengar yoga. He was a very influential teacher in the yoga community.

Proper alignment and balance are the focus in Iyengar yoga. Poses are held for longer periods of time. Props such as mats, blocks and straps etc. are typically used in this practice. Poses are also be held longer in Hatha. Holding the poses for a longer period of time allow for a deeper stretch in order to promote the elongation of the muscles.

Iyengar promotes wellness of the mind and strong focus when moving into each pose. If you are dealing with an injury, this yoga practice allows you to pinpoint that specific area of your body to promote healing. And Iyengar instructor teaches the many aspects of each pose. He or she may note how each movement benefits a specific muscle.

You probably won't break a sweat during an Iyengar class either. Instead, each practice should end with mental clarity and relaxed muscles.

Bikram

You will definitely sweat in a Bikram yoga style class!

Bikram yoga was named after Bikram Choudhury. He developed this yoga style by turning the heat up in the room during class. Sometimes people refer to Bikram as "hot yoga." However, they are two different types of yoga.

Bikram yoga practices the same 26 poses in every class. You will practice those poses over and over again, learning and perfecting each one. The purpose of Bikram yoga is to loosen the muscles by working in a heated atmosphere.

If you plan to attend a Bikram yoga class, consult your instructor if you have been diagnosed with any ailment or sickness. You may need to modify the routine or take short breaks if you begin to feel short of breath or neasous. The temperature in a Bikram class can reach up to 104 degrees. Drink a lot of water, bring a towel and wear clothes that can withstand a heavy amount of sweat.

Ashtanga

K. Pattabhi Jois. brought Ashtanga yoga into the Western culture in the 1970's.

Ashtanga yoga focuses on consistent breathing and movement. This practice teaches you to connect a breathing pattern to the sequence of poses as directed by the instructor. It's purpose is continuous movement while following a very strenuous pace during the poses.

The yoga sequence is the same in each class. It's recommended to sign up for a few beginner classes before committing to an Ashtanga class. This way, you will become more familiar with the simple poses so that you can implement the more difficult poses during each sequence. Ashtanga yoga is designed to keep you moving.

Vinyasa

Vinyasa means to "place something in a special way."

Vinyasa is very similar to Restorative and Ashtanga yoga. The poses are held for a longer period of time. You are given more time to spend placing your body into the correct posture. With each breath, you are able to correct your alignment and balance.

Vinyasa incorporates yoga flow. While each pose is held for a longer period of time, you will still move continuously into the next pose. Depending on the instructor, the poses will most likely change with each class.

Focus is very important in a Vinyasa class. You will need to watch the instructor intently to make sure you are moving correctly into the next position. Although the pace may be slow, it is certainly continuous and can be energized with music.

Yin

Yin is a great class for beginners. In a Yin class, you are given ample amount of time to perfect the poses for proper alignment and balance. You are also in a seated position to hold the poses for 2-5 minutes or more. It's not uncommon in a Yin class to complete only 3-5 poses within an hour. By holding the poses, Yin provides a "stretch to the bone."

This type of stretch not only stretches the muscles, but also loosens and releases the deep connective tissues. These stretch methods provide deeply relaxed muscles by the end of the class.

Meditation is also heavily integrated into a Yin practice. Since it is a slow-paced and quiet atmosphere, the student can integrate meditation into each pose.

Props are utilized in a Yin class as well. Props such as straps and blocks act as extensions of the limbs and provide a deeper stretch. This improves flexibility over time.

Restorative

Ah, Restorative yoga. This level of a yoga practice is typically forgotten, especially in Western culture. We live in a "go-go-go" world and rarely get the option or the ability to slow down.

Most yoga classes will twist and turn your body into those pretzel poses as seen in the books and online. Not Restorative yoga. Restorative-style yoga relaxes and loosens your muscles. This practive gives you the chance to slow down and enter into a peaceful and calm mode of true rest.

Restorative yoga is best practiced in a dark, noiseless and open space. Find space that invites positive feelings and relaxing vibes. Whether your are signing up for a class at the gym or practicing at home, choose the best time of day that works for you. Obviously, make sure that you feel safe in the environment and void of any distractions. Your restorative space should be free of loud noises, cell phones tings and pings and negative energy.

Each pose in restorative yoga session should be used to relax your body. Everyone's body is different. Therefore, your restorative yoga practice should be designed to best fit the way that your body moves and stretches.

Restorative yoga poses are based heavily on props for support. These props assist each part of the body as needed. Extra blankets can cushion areas with added pressure. Bolsters aide in aligning the body and relieving painful stretchs. Straps act as extensions of the arms and legs allowing you to fasten the pose. Blocks support the neck, the back and the knees. Block can also act as landing pieces for hands and feet. You can add as many blankets as needed, folded or unfolded, to support any part of the body.

The great thing about restorative yoga is that you have time! Time to move into the position that feels best for you and your body. You have time to position a prop under, around or on top of your body for comfort.

Restorative is all about support. If your hand is dangling, or if your back is straining, grab a prop. Create your own support with the blocks, bolsters, blankets, etc. If your muscles are strained, they probably aren't being given proper support to ease into the restorative position.

Many times, this type of yoga calls for a very warm atmosphere. Some instructors will even lead you to grab an extra blanket for full body cover. Adding a weighted blanket to your body not only assists gravity in executing the pose, it also generates warmth for you're your muscles. The warmer your muscles are, the safer the stretch becomes.

Socks are also a good idea when practicing restorative yoga. In other yoga classes, you are usually instructed to practice with bare feet. However, in restorative yoga, as mentioned above, warmth is essential. Covering your feet in some form or fashion stops the release of body heat through the toes.

And, here's the kicker. You may fall asleep in a restorative yoga class. The goal is to not fall asleep. But, let's face it – warm air, relaxed muscles, blankets and a quiet room just might do the trick. It's ok. Your instructor will help to wake you properly and safely.

www.ingramcontent.com/pod-product-compliance
Lightning Source LLC
Chambersburg PA
CBHW071625080526
44588CB00010B/1278